ARISTOTLE
AND THE ARC OF
TRAGEDY

OEDIPUS REX, OTHELLO,

DEATH OF A SALESMAN

LEON GOLDEN

PROFESSOR EMERITUS OF CLASSICS
FLORIDA STATE UNIVERSITY

RADIUS
BOOK GROUP

Distributed by Radius Book Group
A Division of Diversion Publishing Corp.
443 Park Avenue South, Suite 1008
New York, NY 10016
www.RadiusBookGroup.com

Library of Congress Control Number: 2017944942

For more information, email info@diversionbooks.com.

First edition: August 2017
Paperback ISBN: 978-1-63576-260-0
eBook ISBN: 978-1-63576-259-4

In Memoriam

O. B. Hardison, Jr.

1928–1990

Scholar   Teacher   Friend

πάντες ἄνθρωποι τοῦ εἰδέναι ὀρέγονται φύσει
All mankind yearn by nature for knowledge.

Aristotle, *Metaphysics* 1.980

CONTENTS

ACKNOWLEDGMENTS

The author gratefully acknowledges permission to use the following copyrighted content:

Martha C. Nussbaum, *The Fragility of Goodness: Luck and Ethics in Greek Tragedy and Philosophy*, 2nd Edition. Copyright © 2001 Martha C. Nussbaum. Reprinted with the Additional: permission of Cambridge University Press.

Excerpt(s) from *Death of a Salesman* by Arthur Miller, copyright 1949, renewed ©1977 by Arthur Miller. Used by permission of Viking Books, an imprint of Penguin Publishing Group, a division of Penguin Random House LLC. All rights reserved.

J. Gassner, "Catharsis and the Modern Theater," in *Aristotle's "Poetics" and English Literature*, ed. Elder Olson (Chicago: University of Chicago Press, 1965), 108–13; essay originally published in *One Act Play Magazine and Theater Review* (August 1937). © 1965 by The University of Chicago Press. All rights reserved. Published 1965. Printed in the United States of America. Used by permission of University of Chicago Press.

Aristotle's Poetics: A Translation and Commentary for Students of Literature. Translated by Leon Golden and commentary by O. B. Hardison, Jr. Gainesville: University Press of Florida, 1982. Used by permission of University Press of Florida.

1

ARISTOTLE'S THEORY OF TRAGEDY

All mankind yearn by nature for knowledge.

Aristotle, *Metaphysics* 1.980

The elegantly simple, impressively profound comment by Aristotle in his *Metaphysics* is, I propose, the necessary basis for understanding the essential argument of his influential treatise on poetic theory, the *Poetics*. This seminal work is still treated with scholarly reverence and cited as a doctrinal authority on matters literary. However, it is imperfectly or seriously misunderstood regarding one or more concepts of the greatest significance, which it places before us as instruments of interpretation.

Two causes appear to have brought poetry into existence and these are natural causes. For the process of *mimesis*[1] is natural to mankind from childhood on and it is in this way that human beings differ from other animals, because they are the most imitative of them and achieve their first learning experiences through *mimesis*. A proof of this is what really happens; for there are some things which are painful to us when we see them but we take pleasure in viewing the most precise representations of them, for example, the forms of the most despised wild animals and of corpses. The reason for this is that the act of learning is not only most pleasant to philosophers but, in a similar way, to everyone else, only others share in this pleasure to a more limited degree. For it is because of this that we take pleasure when we see representations because it turns out that in our viewing of them we learn and infer what each thing is, for example "that this is that" (*Poetics*, 1448 b 4–17).

Aristotle's apparently enigmatic phrase "that this is that" is persuasively explained by Bywater as follows: "Our pleasure in the contemplation of a picture or other work of imitative art is explained here to be the natural concomitant of an intellectual act, the discovery or recognition on our part of the meaning of the picture."[2]

The essential core in witnessing all imitative representations is then for Aristotle a cognitive event, a learning experience. There are in addition other common elements that Aristotle has observed that specifically define over the long arc of representations of the tragic some permanent and unchanging aspects of the human condition. Reformulated time and time again, these elements accurately define the role Aristotelian tragedy plays in human experience. Let us begin with that central figure often designated as the "tragic hero," who is the principal agent in the operation of the tragic action. Aristotle defines the "tragic hero" as follows:

There remains the person whose character lies in between those who are of exceptional virtue and those who are afflicted with very great evil. Such a person is neither preeminent in virtue nor falls into misfortune because of vice and depravity. But rather because of some *hamartia*[3] . . . . It is necessary for the good plot to have a single rather than a double ending, as some people say, and for the change of fortune to take place, not to good fortune from bad fortune, but just the opposite, from good to bad fortune, and not because of depravity but because of some significant *hamartia* on the part of such a person who has been described or on the part of a better rather than a worse one (*Poetics* 1453 a 7–17).

For Aristotle, then, the center of our attention in the unfolding of the mimetic examination of tragic experience is a very specific kind of human being, one whose involvement in tragic circumstances is caused by a very specific kind of failing, a *hamartia* (Gk. ἁμαρτία). Exactly what this critical term designates has been much discussed and variously interpreted whenever tragedy as a genre has appeared on the scene. But my argument in this treatise will be that any tragedy that authentically earns the designation of an "Aristotelian" tragedy requires that this term be understood in one specific way as described below by Gregory Crane:

An example from the study of ancient Greek attitudes illustrates the problems of linguistic interpretation. Aristotle, in the *Poetics* (1453 a 10), writes that the hero in a tragedy suffers disaster because of a *hamartia*. For at least 500 years, *hamartia* was understood as a moral error and gradually became crystallized as the "tragic flaw" of character. This interpretation cannot be maintained in the light of what Aristotle elsewhere says about *hamartia* (Lucas 1968: 299–307), for he clearly uses this term as miscalculation or failure of judgment without moral implications of any kind, but because the Greek term *hamartia* was understood to designate a moral failing and because most scholars through the early 20th century expected classical texts to reinforce Christian ethics, this reading was not seriously challenged. The interpretation of a single word stood as the cornerstone for a complex reading of Greek (and other tragedy). Sophocles' *Oedipus Rex* became trivialized into an unambiguous morality play wherein the proud and irascible Oedipus, deceived by the fatal flaw of pride, meets the fate that he richly deserves.[4]

Crane here gives a succinct and persuasive justification why the all-too-common attempt to find a moral failure, a "tragic flaw" in the *Oedipus Tyrannus* specifically (but also in certain other tragedies) is itself a flawed enterprise.

Bywater had pointed out much earlier that:

hamartia in the Aristotelian sense of the term is a mistake or error of judgement and the deed done in consequence of it is a *harmatema*. In the *Ethics* an *harmatema* is said to originate not in vice or depravity but in ignorance of some material fact or circumstance. This ignorance we are told in another passage takes the deed out of the class of voluntary acts and enables one to forgive or even pity the doer . . . . It is strange that the *hamartia* . . . of which Aristotle is speaking should have been taken . . . by others to mean not an error of judgment, but some ethical fault or infirmity of character . . . . The Sophoclean Oedipus is a man of hasty temper but his *hamartia* was not in that, but in the "great mistake" he made when he became unwittingly the slayer of his own father.[5]

D. W. Lucas confirms the above interpretations of *hamartia* when he writes, "This flaw or frailty is a popular starting point for the discussion of not only Greek Plays. But though *hamartia* can mean many things, there are few, if any, passages where 'flaw' is a justifiable rendering and there can be little doubt that what A. recommends is a character neither very good nor very bad who makes a mistake."[6]

The central figure of an Aristotelian tragedy must then be one who, morally speaking, manifests a significant degree of virtue (Gk. *aretē*)[7] and thus can be recognized as a good (Gk. *spoudaios*)[8] human being whose tragic fall from happiness to misery is not caused by vice or depravity but by some cognitive error or miscalculation (Gk. *hamartia*). Because the error is cognitive and not moral the requisite conditions are established that allow us to experience *pity* and *fear* (defined further in the following paragraph), which Aristotle has decreed to be the central emotional experiences of tragedy. With these concepts understood, we are prepared by Aristotle for achieving the ultimate goal of the human encounter with tragic mimesis (and all forms of artistic mimesis), achieving the cognitive pleasure of a deeper understanding of the human condition. This cognitive pleasure in Aristotelian tragedy is a function of a process designated as catharsis (Gk. *katharsis*). This term was long in wide use by readers and scholars but subject to interpretations that often are at variance with each other. Even more importantly, they reflect a position that is alien to the goal of "learning and inference" (Gk. *manthanein kai syllogizesthai*; see 1448 b 12–17), which Aristotle emphatically asserts is the supreme goal of mankind's interaction with mimetic activity. In the ensuing chapters I offer a summary and analysis of this troubled but critical issue with the hope of offering a persuasive resolution of it.

Pity and *fear* in the *Poetics* are conceptually not very different in meaning from our contemporary use of those terms.

Pity refers to the compassion we feel for the undeserved misfortune of another person, and fear describes the apprehension we experience when we view that undeserved misfortune befalling someone like ourselves. There is one other important qualification that Aristotle makes about the pity and fear that is required for tragedy. The *hamartia* (miscalculation or error) of the tragic hero must result in a destructive act of violence that inflicts undeserved misfortune on someone *closely related* to that tragic hero, and we must feel that circumstances would reasonably make it possible that *someone like ourselves* could have become the victim of that act of violence. It is the range of experience covered by these two terms qualified in this way that forms the content of Aristotelian tragedy.

Because Aristotle did not provide a precise definition of tragic catharsis, it was left to later scholars to offer explanations of the term. It was Jacob Bernays's theory that Aristotle used catharsis in the *Poetics* to express the same meaning the term had in the *Politics*, a very different work of his. In this latter book, the term designated the "purgation" of unwanted or undesirable emotional experiences (such as pity and fear) is based on a direct analogy with the practice of Greek physicians who used purgatives to rid the body of unwanted or undesirable agents causing physical illness. Bywater explains Bernays's theory as follows:

> With some adaptation of the statements and hints [in the *Politics*] thus interpreted, it is not difficult to recover the outlines at any rate of the Aristotelian theory of the cathartic effect of Tragedy: Pity and fear are elements in human nature, and in some men . . . they are present in a disquieting degree. With these latter the tragic excitement is a necessity; but it is also in a certain sense good for all. It serves as a sort of medicine, producing a *catharsis* to lighten and relieve the

soul . . . of the accumulated emotion within it; and as the relief is wanted, there is always a harmless pleasure attending the process of relief.[9]

Over time several other interpretations of Aristotelian catharsis have been put forward by scholars and critics, but none have completely overridden Bernays's medical theory. The purification theory of catharsis is one that has competed, not very successfully, with the purgation theory. This theory asserts that when an audience is exposed either to too much or too little pity and fear (or similar emotions) a process is required (i.e., catharsis) for refining the amount of these emotional experiences so that only a proper degree of them is made available to an audience. Many have found this interpretation unacceptable because no persuasive mechanism has been suggested for achieving this goal. In the latter half of the twentieth century a "cognitive" interpretation of Aristotle's powerful concept has gained momentum and increasing validation by a number of scholars, and it is this cognitive view that guides my interpretation of Aristotle in this study.[10]

Next I wish to cite one of the strongest objections that has been raised against the still influential purgation theory of catharsis. To this statement we append citations from the work of several influential scholars and critics, which provide support for the more recently developed cognitive theory. Gerald Else has written:

And there is another objection to Bernays' interpretation, which would long since have been recognized as fatal if the authority of the *Politics* passage had not been accepted as beyond dispute. His interpretation, no matter how adapted or refined is inherently and indefeasibly *therapeutic*. It presupposes that we come to the tragic drama (unconsciously, if you will) as patients to be cured, relieved, restored to psychic health. But there is not a word to support this in the *Poetics,* not a hint that the end of the drama is to cure or alleviate pathological states. On the contrary it is evident in every line of the work that Aristotle is presupposing *normal* auditors, normal states of mind and feeling, normal emotional and aesthetic experience.[11]

Pedro Laín Entralgo offers the following analysis: "Only by the recognition do the truth, the inner coherence and the meaning of the plot—a superhuman meaning almost always—become evident in the mind of the spectator. The *anagnōrisis* (recognition) represents, in short, the triumph of that deep demand for expression and clarification of the human destiny—a figurative, verbal expression and clarification—that in the face of every possible purely musical and Dionysiac interpretation beats deep within the breast of Attic tragedy. The *Poetics* calls this 'resolution' of the affective state of the spectator *katharsis*."[12]

Kurt von Fritz offers the following insightful account of catharsis: "The catharsis of emotions is not the only essential effect of tragedy; or rather: catharsis does not have only an emotional side. Tragedy according to Aristotle's view is also 'more philosophical,' that means, conducive to a deeper insight than history. Its cognitive function is just as important as its emotional effect. Both are inseparable from one another . . . . [with tragedy providing] an insight into what is universal, the universal circumstances of the human condition" (translation mine).[13]

Donald Keesey notes that for the influential drama scholar and critic John Gassner (whose interpretation of catharsis we cite at greater length later), "without enlightenment there is no tragedy, only melodrama: '. . . enlightenment is not only the third element in catharsis, but the decisive one. The ultimate relief comes when the dramatist brings the tragic struggle to a state of rest . . . . Only enlightenment, a clear comprehension of what was involved in the struggle, an understanding of cause and effect, a judgment on what we have witnessed, and an induced state of mind that places it above the riot of passion—can affect this necessary equilibrium."[14]

O. B. Hardison, Jr., in arguing persuasively for a cognitive interpretation of catharsis, catalogs several prominent aesthetic judgments that give material support to the interpretation of the term as "intellectual clarification":

> A tragedy should be made totally intelligible; the pleasure derived from it is learning; and the pleasure of learning ulti- mately absorbs the pity and fear aroused by the action. The doctrine is perhaps related to such contemporary aesthetic theories as James Joyce's (and Jacques Maritain's) idea of art as epiphany—a sudden luminous perception of a previously hidden set of relations; to Benedetto Croce's concept of aesthetic pleasure as the awareness of coherence; and to the Jungian view of the aesthetic experience as a sudden "insight" into the archetypal range of experience. All these doctrines share with Aristotle the notion of art as learning and the notion of learning as pleasure.[15]

Aristotle's theory of tragedy provides a persuasive defense of the importance of literature, and in particular the literary genre of tragedy, in the lives of mankind over a chronological arc of many centuries. It is mankind's destiny to confront the complex- ities of existence without adequate strategies for subduing them. Still there are deep lessons to be learned about the human con- dition and the disasters that may lie in wait for it in the ongoing struggle for survival. Not all lives reach the pinnacle of anguish that tormented Oedipus, Othello, and Willy Loman but enough of it is present universally that we may consider all of us to be potentially tragic heroes in a major or minor key.

OEDIPUS REX:
AN ICONIC GREEK TRAGEDY

> Approach—consent to embrace me afflicted as I am.
> Trust me; do not feel terror for of all mortals no one
> except myself is vulnerable to my oppressive doom.
>
> *Oedipus Rex*, 1413–15

Before examining relevant details about the specific character of the tragic structure of the *Oedipus Rex* we need to deal with the most important issue of all relating to this, one of the most famous of all tragedies in the canon of the Western literary tradition. It is factually true that in this play Sophocles "created a masterpiece that in the eyes of posterity has overshadowed every other achievement in the field of ancient drama."[16] For some time the fascination of Freud and other psychoanalysts with its theme of patricide and a son's marriage with his mother excited the relevance of the play to an important feature of psychoanalytical theory. Yet, as R. D. Dawe has pointed out, "there must be some reason why this play has also evoked such a powerful and long-lasting fascination on the human mind" for compelling, orthodox literary reasons.[17] One such reason is suggested by Dawe in the following citation from a second Oedipus play by Sophocles written after *Oedipus Rex* and produced posthumously in 401 BCE:

> But there is one prime piece of evidence, which even if it comes from a later play, does at least come from the author himself writing about the same hero. It cannot be left unheard (*Oed. Col.* 962 ff.) [Oedipus here is speaking in the *Oedipus at Colonus* in defense of the patricide and incest he committed in the *Oedipus Rex*]: "The killing and the marriage and all my misfortunes were things that I had to endure, alas, against my will. It was the way the gods wanted it, angry perhaps with my family from times past. So far as I myself am concerned, you could not find any offence to reproach me with that led me to do these deeds against myself and my kin. Tell me this: If a divine oracle was given to my father, to the effect that he was to die at his son's hand, how can you properly make that into any fault of mine, seeing that my father had yet done nothing to give me birth, nor my mother either? At the time, I was *unborn*. And if later my ruin became manifested, as it did, and I fought with and killed my father, not knowing what it was that I was doing, and who it was I was doing it to—how can you reasonably blame me for this act, which was nothing that I intended?"[18]

Oedipus goes on to point out that marriage with Jocasta was again something done in total ignorance, on both sides, of the reality of the situation.

It is clear that Sophocles pondered the profound existential situation he had created in the first Oedipus play, the *deeply ironic suffering of an innocent man for the gravest of all crimes,* and wrestled with the issue of why cosmic forces have allowed or designed *innocent suffering* a role in the fabric of human existence. Finally, he felt able to offer, in the framework of a religious mystery, his response to a theme, *innocent suffering,* that remains troublingly unresolved in iconic works of literature, philosophy, and theology over the many centuries that have followed the appearance of Sophocles's two Oedipus plays.

Any view that Sophocles portrays the gods acting with arbitrary cruelty in *Oedipus Rex* (as they do toward humanity in the *Iliad* and elsewhere in Greek literature) would have to be rejected because of the way the playwright deals with Oedipus's destiny in the successor play to the *Oedipus Rex, Oedipus at Colonus* where, one critic writes, "the crux of this play is the transformation of Oedipus from blind outcast to superhumanly powerful hero."[19] A provocative mystery remains for us, who have been the recipients of the gift of Sophocles's great dramas, to discern meaning behind the way the gods first cruelly plunge Oedipus into the greatest degradation without explanation in *Oedipus Rex* and then, without explanation, elevate him to heroic status in *Oedipus at Colonus,* a thoughtful, premeditated return to the unresolved issues of the earlier play.

From the fifth century BCE, when Sophocles's *Oedipus Rex* was written, to the present, this play has embodied for many readers and critics the fulfillment of the goal of representing an ideal Aristotelian tragic hero within an iconic Aristotelian tragedy. It accomplishes this by operating effectively within a framework that has come to be known as *dramatic, or tragic, irony*: Dramatic irony depends on the structure of a work along with the use of words. In plays it often is created by the audience's awareness of a fate in store for the characters, of which they themselves are unaware.[20]

The opening scene of the *Oedipus Rex* is an eloquent initiation into, and demonstration of, *tragic irony*. In the play's first scene in front of Oedipus's palace the priest of Zeus and a large group of children await the appearance of the king to plead for his intervention in alleviating the plague from which they are suffering badly. Eager to express a willing alliance with his suffering people Oedipus says, "I know that you are all sick and although you are sick there is not anyone of you whose sickness equals mine" (59–61). The surface meaning of what Oedipus communicates by these words is clearly "your grief affects each one of you separately by himself and no one else. But my soul grieves for the city and me and you all together" (63–64). Oedipus alludes here to the huge *quantitative* burden he carries for his people and kingdom that dwarfs the individual pain of each of his subjects. But the original audience for the play was aware, just as we are aware, that the real burden that he bears is a grievous *existential* one arising from an earlier encounter at three crossroads where he unwittingly slew his own father, Laius. Oedipus assures his people that he has taken the one measure he could think of in this perilous situation by sending his brother-in-law, Creon, to the shrine of the god of prophecy, Apollo, to seek advice as to how to proceed against the plague that has descended upon them.

When Creon appears on the scene, he reports the news he has brought from the god Apollo, that the source of the plague from which they are suffering is a pollution that has fallen upon the land because their former king Laius had been murdered and will not be lifted until his murderers have been found and vengeance taken on them. When Oedipus hears the name

"Laius," the former king of the land, he says in all innocence "having heard of him I know who he is, but I have never seen him" (105). Nothing could be more ironic than this line, for Oedipus saw Laius when he was born and later when he killed him. The overall irony is compounded when Creon reports that the one eyewitness to the murder of Laius fled in fear when he returned to the city and found Laius's murderer, Oedipus, on the throne and fled in terror after having falsely reported that it was a band of robbers who had killed Laius not one man alone. At this point, Oedipus intensifies the ironic structure of the play with the following commitment that he makes regarding Laius: "you will see me as an ally in taking vengeance on behalf of this land and at the same time for the god. For it will not be for a distant friend that I will remove this pollution but for my own benefit since whoever it was who killed him might wish to take vengeance on me and so by coming to his aid I will act in my own interest" (135–41). The irony develops further when Oedipus unwittingly places a curse upon himself when he says, "And I curse the one who committed this crime whether it is one man who has escaped detection or one who acted with accomplices, that he wear out his worthless life miserably and I pray that if he lives in my house with my knowledge that I suffer the same fate that I have just now called upon others"; and he concludes with the ironic promise that he will now fight on behalf of Laius "as if he were my own father" (264–65). We see the crushing burden of the irony of human existence now falling heavily on Oedipus's shoulders.

So far Oedipus's behavior is beyond reproach. He is the virtuous (Gk. *spoudaios*) king who responds with sympathy and firm determination to the serious troubles besetting his people and begins to search for clues to the identity of the murderer of the former king. He is advised by Creon, his brother-in-law, that the blind prophet, Teiresias, would be a reliable source of information that no other ordinary human being might possess; Oedipus eagerly accepts this advice and summons the prophet to his presence so that he might interrogate him. Teiresias arrives but immediately demonstrates an unwillingness to provide the information Oedipus wants since it would require him to accuse the king himself of being the actual murderer of his father. Enraged by Teiresias's unwillingness to speak, Oedipus rashly charges him with reluctance to name the murderer because the prophet, himself, is guilty of complicity in the slaying of Laius. Oedipus's anger kindles the wrath of Teiresias who angrily responds to the king: "I say that you are murderer of the man whose murderer you are seeking to find" (362). That response explosively ignites the fury of Oedipus who then accuses Creon, as well as Teiresias, of being part of a conspiracy against him. Finally, Teiresias completes the disastrous message that Oedipus had provoked him to deliver by abandoning him with the catastrophic prophecy that he will soon discover that he is not only the actual murderer of the former king, Laius, but also his son. Further, he is not only the husband of that king's wife, Jocasta, but also her son as well, and that he is both brother and father to the children he has begotten in his marriage with Jocasta.

Creon then appears on the scene and meets with Oedipus's angry charges that he is a conspirator against him with Teiresias. Their bitter quarrel, which leads to the threat of death against Creon, is interrupted by the mediation of Jocasta and the chorus which dissuades Oedipus from proceeding with any violent action against Creon, but which sets the stage for a new and most destructive irony that clouds Oedipus's obscure history and places a shadow on his future destiny. This occurs through

Jocasta's attempt to convince him at this critical moment that it was impossible for him to have slain Laius as charged by Teiresias (707–25) for the following reason: She informs Oedipus that an oracle had come earlier to the city stating that Laius was fated to die at the hands of a son who was to be born to the marriage of Jocasta and Laius. Within three days of that son's birth however, Jocasta tells Oedipus that Laius had that child, ankles bound together, hurled to his death by the hands of others onto an impassable mountain. To reassure Oedipus further, Jocasta says that when Laius was murdered the report came back that it was a band of foreign robbers (casually including the location) "at the crossing point of three roads" who had slain him and so, she says, Apollo did not bring it about that Laius's son was the killer of his father nor that Laius suffered the terrifying crime he feared at the hand of his own child. Oedipus, instead of being relieved by Jocasta's word, is horrified. The brief phrase designating the location of Laius's murder "at the crossing point of three roads" (716) brings about a troubled "frenzy in his soul and a disturbance in his mind." Oedipus then asks further questions about the time and place of Laius's death and the answers begin the grim process of unraveling the dark history of his unwitting crimes against his family. Oedipus is told that the death occurred at a place where there was a crossing point of three roads in Phocis that meet at the same point, one branch coming from Delphi and another leading from Daulis. Further Jocasta says Laius's death was proclaimed to the city just before Oedipus appeared and became the ruler of Thebes in Laius's place. Oedipus then asks about Laius's age and physical appearance and is told the disturbing news that although he was older than Oedipus with graying hair, his appearance was not very distant from Oedipus's own. Then, Oedipus asks for a description of the party that attended

Laius and is told there was a total of five including a herald and that the king rode in a single wagon. It now becomes pressing for Oedipus to get to the absolute truth about the details of the slaying of Laius. It happens that there was one eyewitness to the altercation at the three crossroads, a slave, who after he told his story to Jocasta and found Oedipus occupying the slain king's throne begged the queen to send him far from the city into the country, which she gladly did. It now becomes urgent for Oedipus to interrogate this eyewitness in person and find exoneration from, or condemnation for, the devastating fate that had shadowed his existence before he met with and slew an angry man of royal stature just prior to arriving at Thebes.

By line 771 it becomes a necessity for Oedipus to tell the difficult story of how he came to be at the fateful crossing of three roads when Laius and Oedipus, unknown to each other, met in a fatal conflict. Oedipus explains that his father was Polybus of Corinth and he, Oedipus, was raised as the son and heir to the Corinthian kingdom. One evening a drunken man taunted Oedipus as not being the actual son of Polybus and though his father vehemently denied the insult, the incident continued on to disturb Oedipus. Thus, without the knowledge of his parents, he went to the prophetic shrine of Apollo to ask for divine clarification of his parentage. There the god refused him the knowledge he sought, but gave him the horrifying prophecy that he would commit incest with his mother and become the murderer of the father who had begotten him. At this point, Oedipus abandoned his homeland of Corinth forever to defeat the fulfillment of this abhorrent oracle. On his way from distancing himself from Corinth, he tells Jocasta, he came upon a party of travelers such as the one that has been described as traveling with Laius. Oedipus and the travelers confronted each other and the party with Laius, including the old man himself, tried to thrust Oedipus aside from blocking their path on the road. At this show of violence Oedipus says he struck the chariot driver in anger and in turn, as he was passing the chariot itself, the old man riding in it, watching, as Oedipus approached him, came down with his double whip "squarely on the middle of [his] head (809) but [for that blow] he paid a much heavier price. To tell it simply, struck by the walking stick in my hand he rolled backward straight out of the middle of the chariot and then I killed them all" (810–13). In offering this confession the burden of guilt Oedipus feels does not, in another ironic twist of fortune, come close to the existential disaster actually afflicting him. His first surmise is that a disastrous fate may have befallen him because of the possibility that there might have been some relationship between the stranger he killed at the three crossroads and King Laius. If this were the case, then Oedipus realizes he might have inadvertently called down the severest of curses upon himself that he had earlier proclaimed against the unknown killer of Laius when he first learned of the king's death and had no suspicion of any possible involvement of himself in that event. In these circumstances, he asks who of mankind would be more pitiful, more god-hated than he, ironically not perceiving the abyss of degradation still awaiting him.

Oedipus tells Jocasta that all now depends on the accuracy of the report of the slave who had witnessed the killing of Laius and then asked to be sent far from the city of Thebes when he returned there and found Oedipus occupying Laius's throne. If the eyewitness repeats the story that a band of robbers killed Laius, then Oedipus is innocent of Laius's death, for he was traveling alone when the confrontation with the king's party took place. Jocasta assures him that was the original story and reminds him that the prophecy that Laius would be slain by his son had to be false because that child she says had been exposed in the wilderness to die long before King Laius had been killed.

The web of irony twists more tightly around Oedipus when a messenger from Corinth arrives to summon him home to his city of origin to replace Polybus who has died on the throne of that city. At first Oedipus and Jocasta are cheered by this news as it appears to remove the onus of guilt for the murder of Laius from Oedipus's shoulders. But when Oedipus refuses to return to Corinth because he fears to fulfill the oracle's warning that he is destined for an unholy marriage with his mother, the unwinding net of irony springs a further trap. The messenger attempts to persuade him that he has nothing to fear from returning to Corinth because neither Polybus nor Merope were his real parents. Rather, it was he, the messenger says, who long years past, had been a shepherd in the narrow valleys of Mt. Cithaeron where a neighboring shepherd, a servant of Laius, gave him a child to adopt as his own, a child who had been exposed and injured in the fields. In the net of irony enclosing fast upon Oedipus that other shepherd turns out to be the same person who had been ordered by Laius and Jocasta to expose the child, was the only surviving eyewitness to the slaughter of Laius and his party at the three cross roads, and has also just now been summoned by Jocasta to give testimony about that event to Oedipus.

When Jocasta hears that the servant of Laius who was originally ordered to carry out the death sentence on the child, Oedipus, had not done so but, pitying the child, had delivered him for safety into the hands of a Corinthian shepherd, she begins, suddenly, horrifyingly, to solve the riddle of Oedipus's existence. Oedipus presses on to find the identity of the servant of Laius who would have handed him over as an injured child to the Corinthian shepherd. Those assembled say that it was the very person Jocasta has summoned, the surviving eyewitness of Laius's murder. Now Jocasta knows with absolute certainty the terrible destiny of her son/husband and she begs him to go no further in the search for the truth about his origins, but he angrily rejects her warning and proudly insists on uncovering the dark secret at the core of his existence that so far has eluded him. In the final irony he endures before the true picture of disaster unfolds, he deludes himself by believing that Jocasta's warning to desist from his search for the truth about his origins is based on her woman's pride, her misplaced fear that she will be made to feel shame, because his birth will prove to be humble and not royal. To this supposed arrogant thought on her part Oedipus presents his proud rebuttal, the irony of ironies, that he considers himself to be the child of "good fortune" and with such a mother as that granting him her favors, he will not be dishonored. Oedipus then presses the recalled servant for the truth about how he as a child had first come into possession of the Corinthian messenger, and learns the abysmal truth that the servant had received him from Jocasta herself with the order to carry out a death sentence on the child because prophecies had been received that the child would kill its parents. In answer to Oedipus's question as to why he had given the child to the Corinthian shepherd instead of carrying out his instructions to kill it, he replies, because he pitied the child and thought that the Corinthian would remove it to safety in the foreign land from which he came.

This approaches the final crushing experience for Oedipus as he realizes that the whole sordid story of his existence would now become clear and wishes that he may now look upon the light for the last time in his life since he was damned in his birth, damned in his marriage, and damned in the lives he has destroyed. All that is left for him is to find that his wife, Jocasta, has committed suicide by hanging herself and to inflict the final torment upon himself by stripping the sharp golden pins by which her clothing was fastened and, with his head uplifted, use them to strike out his eyes and blind himself. In his profound misery, Oedipus's immediate future is at the end of this play left in the hands of Creon to determine, although as we have noted, Sophocles returned to the question of how we are to interpret the transcendent significance of the Oedipus myth in the final play he wrote and that was staged posthumously, *Oedipus at Colonus*. It remains for us, however, to define now the specific characteristics that define the tragic nature of *Oedipus Rex* as an independently existing drama that has achieved preeminence in the canon of Western literature.

OEDIPUS AS TRAGIC HERO: THE QUESTION OF *HAMARTIA*

We have seen that Aristotle's theory of tragedy explicitly requires that the tragic hero be a person who is neither exceptional in virtue (Gk. *aretē*) and justice, nor one who falls into misfortune through evil and depravity, but someone in between these extremes whose downfall is caused by error or miscalculation (Gk. *hamartia*). We have also seen in the authoritative discussions of *hamartia* (reviewed in chapter 1), offered by such scholars as Crane, Bywater, and Lucas, that the term was used by Aristotle in the *Poetics* to refer to an *intellectual and not a moral* error or miscalculation. Nevertheless, in the long history of the interpretation of the Oedipus story, and still widely today, critics have found ways of attributing some form of moral or tragic flaw to Oedipus to transform the drama into a morality play, where some deeply embedded guilt or "sin" on his part would justify the extremity of suffering that had become the destined goal of his existence. Most often the tragic flaw attributed to Oedipus is the intense anger that he exhibited when he fiercely retaliated and killed the hostile party (including Laius) who confronted him at three crossroads, and the angry threats, not carried out, he made against Creon and Teiresias when words or actions on their part suggested the yet unsuspected, horrifying destiny to which he was doomed. Describing the *Oedipus Rex* as a play about the tragic flaw of intemperate wrath, I believe, completely subverts the power, meaning, and influence of this world-class tragedy. A persuasive and potent corrective view is offered by E. R. Dodds for our guidance, in his insightful account of Oedipus's character and actions:

> what fascinates us is the spectacle of a man freely choosing, from the highest of motives, a series of actions which lead to his ruin. Oedipus might have left the plague to take its course; but pity for the sufferings of his people compelled him to consult Delphi. When Apollo's word came back, he might still have left the murder of Laius uninvestigated; but pity and justice required him to act. He might not have forced the truth from the reluctant Theban herdsman; but because he cannot rest content with a lie, he must tear away the last veil from the illusion in which he has lived so long. Teiresias, Jocasta, and the herdsman each in turn tries to stop him, but in vain: he must read the last riddle, the riddle of his own life. The immediate cause of Oedipus' ruin is not "Fate" or "the gods"—no oracle said that he must discover the truth—and still less does it lie in his own weakness; what causes his ruin is his own strength and courage, his loyalty to

Thebes and his loyalty to the truth. In all of this we see him as a free agent.[21]

All of the facts cited by Dodds testify to the strength of Oedipus's moral fiber and refute the ascription of a "tragic flaw" to him, as opposed to a "cognitive error or miscalculation" (Gk. *hamartia*). Dodds's further account of the meaning of the play is also important and impressive because it leads us to the required cognitive *hamartia* that must complete the total picture of the Aristotelian tragic hero:

> Certainly the *Oedipus Rex* is a play about the blindness of man and the desperate insecurity of the human condition: in a sense every man must grope in the dark as Oedipus gropes, not knowing who he is or what he has to suffer; we all live in a world of appearance which hides from us who-knows-what dreadful reality. But surely the *Oedipus Rex* is also a play about human greatness. Oedipus is great, not in virtue of a great worldly position—for his worldly position is an illusion which will vanish like a dream—but in virtue of his inner strength; strength to pursue the truth at whatever personal cost, and strength to accept and endure it when found . . . . Oedipus is great because he accepts the responsibility for *all* his acts, including those which are *objectively most horrible, though subjectively innocent* (italics mine.)[22]

> To me personally Oedipus is a kind of symbol of the human intelligence which cannot rest until it has solved all the riddles—even the last riddle, to which the answer is that human happiness is built on an illusion.[23]

Oedipus's *hamartia* is the "universal blindness" clouding and blocking for all mankind a precise and clear vision of its place in the universe, of the reality which surrounds it, of the future which awaits it. The secrets hidden from Oedipus are extreme, but not without a relevant connection to all of us.

OEDIPUS REX AND CATHARSIS

We have noted that three major interpretations of Aristotelian catharsis have developed over time: purgation, purification, and intellectual clarification. In medical purgation, the cathartic goal of tragedy is supposed to be the therapeutic removal, the elimination of painful and disturbing emotions such as pity and fear aroused by tragedy in an audience, in the same way as medical intervention removes unwanted physical illness. In catharsis as purification, tragedy is supposed to refine excess or deficient experiences of unpleasant or painful and disturbing emotions, such as pity and fear, so that the audience experiences only the spiritually and intellectually beneficial degree of those emotions. In catharsis as intellectual clarification, the goal of tragedy aims at providing a significant cognitive experience, a powerful opportunity for learning and making inferences about the nature of the human condition. E. R. Dodds does not explicitly reference the catharsis question, but it is quite clear from his analysis of the *Oedipus Rex* (discussed in the preceding section) that his approach to the reading of the play is to illuminate its cognitive significance, to plunge into the depth of its relevance for the tragic nature of the human condition. Twice in his essay he uses the phrase "the enlargement of our sensibility" to describe what the effect of tragedy should be on a serious and questioning audience. I take that phrase to be synonymous with Aristotle's judgment that the goal of tragic mimesis should be to facilitate "learning and inference" (*Poetics*, 148 b 16) and "learning and inference" precisely define the cognitive function of catharsis in its role as "intellectual clarification."

Oedipus Rex is, then, a preeminent tragedy illuminating the ironic state of the human condition, where a human being is placed, without any taint of guilt, in a situation in which, without knowing or wishing it, he performs actions that are objectively "most horrible," but for which he was "subjectively innocent."[24] Far more commonly in tragedy, protagonists are complicit in actions that bring disaster down upon themselves and others. Moreover, in the *Oedipus Rex* forces are at work in generating the tragic circumstances that are, for the most part, outside of the interactions of human agents such as chance, coincidence, and possible divine intervention.

The history of literary tragedy in the post-classical era reveals a number of works of compelling tragic force. Notable among these, and representing different chronological periods, are *Othello* and *Death of a Salesman*. These dramas will allow an instructive comparative analysis of similarities and differences in tragic achievement with *Oedipus Rex*. Our discussion now turns to these latter two plays. In them, as in most Shakespearean and modern tragedies, recognizable human interactions, not provocative divine mysteries, are critical to the way in which the tragedy unfolds and entraps the principal characters.

III

OTHELLO: AN ICONIC SHAKESPEAREAN TRAGEDY

I kissed thee ere I killed thee. No way but this, killing myself to die upon a kiss.

Othello, act 5, scene 2, 363–64

E. R. Dodds served us as a sure guide, in chapter 2, to the interpretation of the *Oedipus Rex* in an Aristotelian context. Influential Shakespearean scholar A. C. Bradley can in a similar way help us make Aristotelian connections to *Othello* and Shakespearean tragedy in general. Bradley, like many astute students of tragedy, is familiar with the basic doctrines of the Aristotelian theory of tragedy, which he both applies and adapts to his specifically Shakespearean subject matter. Thus, important aspects of his analysis will be familiar to us from our discussion of Aristotelian doctrine in chapter 1. Bradley writes:

> A Shakespearean tragedy as so far considered may be called a story of exceptional calamity leading to the death of a man of high estate. But it is clearly more than this . . . . The calamities of tragedy do not simply happen, nor are they sent; they proceed mainly from actions, and those the actions of men. We see several human beings placed in certain circumstances; and we see, arising from the co-operation of their characters in these circumstances, certain actions. These actions beget other actions and these others beget others again until this series of inter-connected deeds leads by an apparently inevitable sequence to a catastrophe. The effect of such a series on the imagination is to make us regard the sufferings which accompany it, and the catastrophe in which it ends, not only or chiefly as something which happens to the persons concerned, but equally as something which is caused by them. This at least may be said of the principal persons, and among them, of the hero, who always contributes in some measure to the disaster in which he perishes . . . . The "story" or "action" of a Shakespearean tragedy does not consist, of course, solely of human actions or deeds; but the deeds are the predominant factor . . . . The center of the tragedy, therefore, may be said with equal truth to lie in action issuing from character, or in character issuing in action.[25]

OTHELLO AS TRAGIC HERO: THE QUESTION OF *HAMARTIA*

Before addressing the trajectory of events in the play that lead

Othello from proud, heroic dominance to fatal self-destruction, I want to call attention to some comments that Bradley makes about the tragic hero. His ideas are evocative of Aristotelian criteria for the character of the tragic hero, or remind us of Oedipus's stature in such a role. Bradley speaks of the magnitude that the hero must have, "which stirs not only sympathy and pity, but admiration, terror and awe," and he notes that the hero's "tragic trait which is also his greatness, is fatal to him."[26] He further confirms that "In most cases, the tragic error involves no breach of right; in some (e.g., that of Brutus or Othello), it is accompanied by a full conviction or right," and he speaks of the tragic error that "the comparatively innocent hero still shows as some marked imperfection or defect that can even take the form of 'genius' in some like Hamlet and Cleopatra but others like Othello, Lear, Macbeth, Coriolanus, are built on the grand scale; and, desire, passion, or will attains in them a terrible force . . . . a fatal tendency to identify the whole being with one interest, object, passion, or habit of mind. This, it would seem, is, for Shakespeare the fundamental tragic trait . . . . it is a fatal gift but it carries with it a touch of greatness; and when there is joined to it nobility of mind, or genius, or immense force, we realize the full power and reach of the soul."[27] In Bradley's view what he calls the hero's "tragic trait" is not a profound moral flaw but reflects some kind of mistake or miscalculation in his interaction with others. The following comment by Bradley sums up his view of Othello as an authentic tragic hero: "This character is so noble, Othello's feelings and actions follow so inevitably from it and from the forces brought to bear on it—and his sufferings are so heart-rending, that he stirs, I believe, in most readers a passion of mingled love and pity which they feel for no other hero in Shakespeare."[28] Note that the tragic hero bears the stigma of *hamartia* as that term is defined in Aristotle's *Poetics*: the capacity for making serious miscalculations and errors, but not guilty of a moral flaw or sin.

We saw that the critical factor in our moral judgment of Oedipus was that his actions (encompassing murder and incest) were *objectively horrifying but subjectively innocent* within the context of extreme challenges to his integrity and moral fiber, to which he responded always within the wide range of his nobility of character. For this reason we identified his actions as the result of a humanly unavoidable cognitive error or miscalculation and not a tragic flaw or moral sin.

Shakespeare builds the case slowly and carefully for both Othello's claim to the status of tragic hero and his vulnerability to a fatal cognitive *hamartia*. First his warrior status is established as the Duke of Venice and the assembled senators impatiently await Othello's response to their summons to take command of their naval forces to ward off a powerful Turkish fleet bent on subduing Cyprus. It is clear that the highest powers governing Venice are unhesitatingly placing the welfare of their state in the hands of Othello, who shows himself eager and confident to take on the heavy responsibilities offered him. Against this background of a serious crisis facing the state of Venice, in act 1 Shakespeare plays off the origins of the love affair between Othello and Desdemona. This introduces the audience to the exotic dimension of Othello's character, which Desdemona finds irresistible. She is mesmerized by his stories of military adventures, of capture by an insolent foe and having been sold into slavery, and having been redeemed from slavery, of his having visited strange and mysterious places on the Earth, of meeting with "cannibals who eat each other, the anthropophagi, and men whose heads grow beneath their shoulders" (1.3.142–45). This impressively adventurous side of

Othello's life opens the experience of romantic love to Othello that had never been a possibility for someone like him, who had been sustained exclusively by outstanding military exploits, the glory and danger of war. Nevertheless, it also provides the dark arena for his downfall as it becomes the tormenting psychological vulnerability exploited by Iago for achieving malicious vengeance against the noble Moor.

From now on our focus will be on a quartet of players, Othello, Iago, Desdemona, and Cassio. Their interaction with one another releases the strong currents of mutual involvement that, in Bradley's words, represent the "centre" of a Shakespearean tragedy where action issues from character or character issues in action to become the determinative course which a tragedy takes on its way to an ultimate climax.

As act 1 of the play comes to an end the necessary requirements for the unfolding of the drama are in place; Othello and Desdemona set out separately for the conflict that is raging against the Turkish assault on Cyprus. Othello arranges with the Duke that Desdemona will follow him to the war zone under care and escort of Iago, his ancient, a man whom he describes as of "honesty and trust" (1.3.285). Thus, before the end of Act I Shakespeare provides a subtle indication of Othello's naive but fatal misconception about the character of Iago, which thereby lays the foundation for his own tragic fate. Skillfully Shakespeare reinforces the portrait of a treacherous Iago immediately in the Act's final scene. There Iago wrestles Roderigo into submission to his warped and diabolical plot against Othello by playing upon Roderigo's foolish, totally unrealistic passion for Desdemona as Iago pretends to enter a conspiracy with Roderigo to accomplish his own delusional goal. As Roderigo expresses pessimism about his possible success in winning Desdemona for himself, Iago keeps pressing him to "put money in thy purse" (1.3.344–49) to finance this wildly illusory romantic dream of his, money which Iago of course diverts to his own uses cynically reflecting that "Thus do I ever make my fool my purse" (1.3.389). All this is prelude to the final lines of the Act where Iago outlines to himself the process by which he will unleash his fierce hatred upon Othello and destroy him: he will take advantage of Othello's inexperience of worldly matters unconnected with wars and armies, and his "free and open nature" (1.3.405) to implant a tormenting suspicion in his mind that Cassio "is too familiar" (1.3.402) with Desdemona, a task made all the easier because Cassio "hath a person and smooth dispose to be suspected, framed to make women false" (1.3.404). Iago is so convinced that all parts of his master plan are falling into place so neatly that he boasts to himself that Othello "will as tenderly be led by the nose as asses are" (1.3.407–8).

In act 2, scene 1, Shakespeare slowly and carefully develops Iago's malevolent plot to wreck the humanity of Othello. First, he notes that Cassio warmly welcomes Desdemona to Cyprus, caressing her hand, throwing kisses to her in a courtly way. Iago reflects that "with as little a web as this will I ensnare as great a fly as Cassio" (2.1.168–69). The second stage of his plot involves the further manipulation of Roderigo, whose jealousy and anger he rouses by fabricating a story that Cassio and Desdemona have become lovers. Roderigo says honestly and naively that he saw in their warm mutual greetings only an act of courtesy, to which Iago passionately retorts, "Lechery, by this hand! an index and obscure prologue to the history of lust and foul thoughts" (2.1.262). The power of Iago's rhetoric overcomes Roderigo's weak will and doomed all-consuming desire for Desdemona and he agrees to become his ally in causing an uproar with Cassio at the center of it so that he will be dismissed from Othello's favor. Only in this way, Iago warns the gullible Roderigo, can Cassio be removed as an impediment to his preposterous aspirations directed at Desdemona. With Roderigo in place as a sacrificial foil, Iago, out of a venomous hatred compounded of rage over a disappointed promotion, lust directed at Desdemona, and suspicion of being cuckolded by Othello, is prepared to drive Othello "into a jealousy so strong that judgment cannot cure . . . . [and practice] upon his peace and quiet even to madness" (2.1.309–19).

The following action in act 2, scene 3 is a critical point for the forward progress of Iago's plan to subdue Othello into utter wretchedness. The first step he takes is to exploit Cassio's known vulnerability to alcohol as he accosts him with that dangerous weakness on his mind. The victory over the Turks and the safe arrival of Othello and Desdemona in Cyprus ushers in a time for jubilation, and Iago encourages Cassio to drink to this occasion for celebratory rejoicing. Cassio resists but is trapped by the skillful manipulation of Iago into partaking of additional alcohol and loses his self-control. Then Iago arranges for a party of three gentlemen of Cyprus, whom he has already "flustered with flowing cups" (2.3.60) and who, inflamed with the drinks supplied by Iago, are now even more than ordinarily aggressive in taking offense at challenges to their honor. Now it is Iago's plan "amongst this flock of drunkards" (2.3.61–62) to employ Roderigo to incite a violent brawl involving the three gentlemen of Cyprus, Montano, the governor of Cyprus, and, most importantly, Cassio now the victim of more alcohol than he can handle, at the center of it. By arranging this unseemly explosion of drunken rage, Iago's goal is to achieve the next step in his scheme, creating a serious rift between Cassio and Othello. This he accomplishes by first falsely insinuating to Othello, when he arrives on the scene to halt the drunken melee caused by Iago, that Cassio was responsible for initiating the disturbance. Thus, the angered Othello disciplines

Cassio by delivering his decent and loyal officer the crushing blow of dismissing him as his lieutenant. Now Iago's fiendish design takes on an inexorably cruel momentum as with feigned good will he offers Cassio the plausible but maliciously intended advice to recover favor with Othello by enlisting Desdemona as his ally in overcoming the recently developed hostility between the two men. This strategy appeals very much to Cassio who has earlier been on very good terms with both Othello and Desdemona and has no suspicion of Iago's diabolical plan to destroy Othello by using him, Roderigo, and Desdemona as duped instruments of his vengeance. The crowning point of his scheme now is to insinuate to Othello that any pleading that Desdemona does on behalf of Cassio is based on her sexual attraction to him, "And by how much she strives to do him good, she shall undo her credit with the Moor. So, will I turn her virtue into pitch, and out of her own goodness make the net, that shall enmesh them all" (2.3.371–74).

Starting with act 3, scene 3, Iago begins to unravel the design he has carefully been shaping to incite rage and jealousy in Othello's mind. He starts by subtly inserting into his conversations with Othello innuendo aimed at raising suspicion about Cassio's behavior toward Desdemona. We have seen that Iago has laid the groundwork for the highly subversive effect of this innuendo by encouraging Cassio to press Desdemona into service as the enthusiastic advocate for his return into the good favor of Othello. Based on innocent words and gestures Iago builds a case in Othello's mind for suspecting the motive of Desdemona's urgent, insistent appeals on Cassio's behalf. He grows bold enough to say to Othello, "Look to your wife; observe her well with Cassio . . . . In Venice they do let God see the pranks they dare not show their husbands; their best conscience is not to leave't undone but [keep't] unknown . . . . She did deceive her father, marrying you . . . . Ay, there's the point! as to be bold with you, not to affect many proposed matches, of her own clime complexion and degree, whereto we see in all things nature tends . . . . But, pardon me, I do not in position distinctly speak of her, though I may fear her will, recoiling to her better judgment, may fall to match you with her country forms, and happily repent" (3.3.198–238). Iago has now spoken boldly and cruelly, indeed, and a painful disquiet pervades Othello's soul.

Shakespeare now intensifies Iago's plans with a stroke of accidental fortune that he cynically manipulates to his benefit. In a conversation that Desdemona has with a troubled Othello, she loses a handkerchief, recovered by Emilia, Iago's wife, that had been his first gift to her and from that time on had held a special place in their relationship. Iago had for some time wanted to use it as an instrument in his conspiracy against Othello. Emilia delivers the handkerchief to Iago and now his scheme takes actual shape as he intends to place the handkerchief in Cassio's lodging where it can become, if he acts with sufficient malice and cunning, damning evidence of alleged "infidelity" on the part of Cassio and Desdemona.

Iago's next moves are to incite Othello to greater and greater degrees of jealous, uncontrollable madness. So skillful is he that Othello falls into such a rage as to warn Iago as follows: "Villain, be sure that you prove my love a whore! Be sure of it, give me ocular proof, or by the worth of my eternal soul, thou had best been born a dog than answer my waked wrath" (3.3.360–63). In the secrecy of his dark soul Iago rejoices in his great success in transforming Othello into an agent of undisciplined vengeance and so accelerates his strategy of embittered destruction of another human being by two nefarious actions: first he claims to have heard Cassio crying out in his sleep one night words of illicit passionate love for Desdemona. Then he, describing the handkerchief which Desdemona had lost and he now has stolen, asks Othello if he recognizes it for "[I did] today see Cassio wipe his beard with [it]" (3.3.439). With this earliest and dearest gift which Othello had given to Desdemona now resting in the profane hands of Cassio, thus does Iago deliver the shattering blow to Othello's raging jealousy that brings both of them to their knees to swear the devil's own allegiance to each other to end the lives of two innocent victims. Othello assigns to the all-too-willing Iago the task of dispatching Cassio from this world while he withdraws "to furnish [himself] with some swift means of death for" Desdemona (3.3.478). Their pact concludes with Othello saying to Iago, "now thou art my lieutenant," and Iago replying, "I am your own forever" (3.3.479–80).

In act 3, scene 4, Iago's murderous plan advances further in two steps as Othello, upon meeting Desdemona asks to see his handkerchief, a request with which she cannot comply and later, Cassio, seeing his girlfriend, Bianca, hands her Desdemona's handkerchief and asks her to copy its design so he can duplicate it if he should be asked to return the article. In act 4, scene 1, Iago throws caution to the winds and attacks Othello's emotional vulnerability with all of his diabolical cunning. He taunts Othello with false images and stories of intimacies between Desdemona and Cassio that drives Othello mad with jealous, murderous wrath. He arranges for Othello to observe a conversation he is going to have with Cassio on the subject he alleges of his relationship with Desdemona. Instead, however, with Othello out of hearing range, he introduces the topic of Bianca, someone scorned by Cassio, who enjoys mocking and treating her with sarcasm and scorn even while making use of her for his own purposes in various ways. Iago is fully aware that when the subject of Bianca comes up in Cassio's presence "he . . . . cannot restrain from the excess of laughter" and that as Cassio shall smile "Othello shall go mad; and his unbookish jealousy must conster poor Cassio's smiles, gestures, and light behaviour quite in the wrong" (4.1.99–104). Iago is highly successful in creating a charade that totally traps Othello in the fatal deception he has so carefully designed and under his breath Othello says of Cassio "O! I see that nose of yours, but not that dog I shall throw it to" (4.1.143–44). Iago so deviously escalates the emotional pressure on defenseless Othello that at one point he asks, "How shall I murder him, Iago?" (4.1.173). And a little later, speaking of how to murder Desdemona he says, "Get me some poison, Iago" (4.1.208). To which Iago responds with unrelenting cruelty, "Do it not with poison. Strangle her in her bed, even the bed she hath contaminated" (4.1.212–13). "Good, good! the justice of it pleases. Very good," Othello responds in agony (4.1.214–15).

In act 4, scene 2, the next stage in Iago's unsavory stratagem for wreaking vengeance on Othello unfolds. We first note the decaying self-control that corrupts Othello's behavior toward Desdemona as he charges her with being a whore and offers her no chance to vindicate herself. Then, Iago is confronted by Roderigo who denounces him as a lying deceiver. For Iago claimed to have taken a fortune of jewels from Roderigo with which to corrupt Desdemona into an affair with him, but Roderigo now finds Iago's promised results are empty words that have won him no advantage. He holds himself ready now to demand restitution of his bribery from Desdemona or challenge Iago to a duel to repay his guilty deception. Iago's capacity for evil is not exhausted by this threat to his overall plan and he convinces the gullible Roderigo that they are on the way to accomplishing their goal with only one more step to take: Roderigo must murder Cassio that night and then all will be well. Lust and a dull intellect mar

Roderigo's well-grounded suspicion of Iago's treachery and so he is easily led to his own destruction. Act 4 ends with Desdemona gloomily preparing for her final and fatal encounter with an Othello whose soul and mind have been twisted by Iago into instruments that are no longer capable of dealing with reality.

In the final act of the play (act 5, scene 1) Iago fully disrobes his foul and disgusting soul to us. He opens the scene with the proclamation regarding his incitement to Roderigo to commit murder on his behalf, "Now whether he kill Cassio, or Cassio him, or each do kill each other, every way makes my gain" (5.3.12–14). Iago's plan to create mayhem with Roderigo and Cassio at the center of it scores a partial success with Roderigo wounding Cassio and Iago taking advantage of the situation to kill Roderigo, which eliminates one obstacle to his goal of the total destruction of Othello, Desdemona, and Cassio. In the play's grand climax (act 5, scene 2), Othello confronts Desdemona with his intention to kill her for infidelity to him and offers as proof of her crime the fact that he saw Cassio holding in his hands the handkerchief that he had given her as the initial sign and seal of their deepest love. Desdemona's sincerest affirmations of her steadfast loyalty to Othello fail because he, cunningly misled by Iago, falsely asserts that the essential witness to whom she appeals for corroboration of her innocence, Cassio, is already dead at the hands of Iago.

It is Emilia's appearance on the scene that finally unmasks the monstrous conspiracy of Iago to bring to ruin the lives of three of Shakespeare's most virtuous characters. All that is left is for us is to hear Othello's gigantic cry of woe after Emilia exposes Iago's corrupt web of intrigue: "Will you demand that demi-devil why he hath thus ensnared my soul and body?" (5.3.12–14) and Iago's ghostly criminal response that has echoed through the ages: "Demand me nothing. What you know you know. From this time forth I will never speak word" (5.2.301–2).

In this play, Shakespeare allows neither doubt about Othello's nobility and heroism in the service of the state of Venice, nor of the depth and authenticity of his love for Desdemona. In the final words that Othello speaks, Shakespeare permits him to be his most eloquent advocate: "When you shall these deeds relate, speak of me as I am, nothing extenuate, nor set down aught in malice. Then you must speak of one not easily jealous, but, being wrought, perplexed in the extreme; of one whose hand, like the base Judean threw a pearl away richer than all his tribe" (5.2.339–46).

Othello is the victim of a trap sprung upon him by an evil genius bent on destroying him and others by a pathological hatred and jealously that eludes normal human understanding. Iago himself offers the following diagnosis of Othello's tragic *hamartia*:

> The Moor is of a free and open nature
> that thinks men honest that but seem to be so,
> and will as tenderly be led by the nose
> as asses are.
> I have it. It is engendered! Hell and night
> must bring this monstrous birth to the world's light.
>
> (1.3.405–10)

Like Oedipus, Othello's *hamartia* is what otherwise could be his most impressive virtue, except that it was exploited into a fatal vulnerability by a transgressor so opposite in character to his victim, so driven by venomous hatred, so malevolently adept at pursuing vengeance, that he looms before us as arguably Shakespeare's greatest villain.

OTHELLO AND CATHARSIS

Shakespeare's *Othello* is an impressive template for a theme that is not uncommon in the literature of tragedy: the Aristotelian concept of the fall of a virtuous human being from happiness to misery because of a *hamartia*, an intellectual error, mistake, or miscalculation. We have shown why in the *Poetics* Aristotle carefully employed the term, *hamartia*, as a cognitive error, mistake, or miscalculation, and not as the "tragic or moral flaw" that critics and readers *have* commonly perceived to be operative in many post-classical tragedies. Our discussion demonstrates that, in this play, Iago himself testifies that the virtuous Othello would never have contrived the death of Desdemona if his own vile genius had not corrupted the play's hero. And Othello's deliberate and brave choice of suicide in atonement for the objectively horrible but subjectively innocent murder of Desdemona testifies that he is fully worthy of recognition as an authentic Aristotelian tragic hero, vulnerable to grave human error but completely innocent of despicable mortal sin. Moreover, by *fully assuming* responsibility for his action he also embodies the concept of those impressive Shakespearean heroes, described in the foregoing section by A. C. Bradley, who possess the "magnitude which stirs not only sympathy and pity but admiration, terror, and awe." This is an encomium that both Oedipus and Othello share with equal justification in the conflicting circumstances of good and evil in which their lives were entrapped but from which they escaped. Their escape left them not unscathed, but guiltless victims of the mystery of our mortal destiny, or of the fathomless depravity of a human agent.

In the mid-twentieth century, Arthur Miller created a compelling dramatic work that was explicitly designed to challenge the relevance and thus the preeminence of Greek and Shakespearian tragedies as iconic representations of the nature of tragedy for the modern world. He calls attention to the fact that we no longer have an abundance of kings and royal families to draw upon for a supply of tragic heroes and tragic plots. In their place we have the "common man or woman" such as his hero Willy Loman ("low man"), who out of necessity becomes the emblematic bearer of the title of "tragic hero" in the modern and post-modern eras. The clashing destinies of King Oedipus, Othello the Moor of Venice, and the all-too-symbolic American salesman Willy Loman should prove instructive in our search for the truth about the nature of tragedy.

IV

DEATH OF A SALESMAN: AN ICONIC MODERN TRAGEDY

He had the wrong dreams. All, all, wrong . . . .
He never knew who he was.

Biff in *Death of a Salesman*,
Requiem (final scene of the play)

Contemporary with the opening production of *Death of a Salesman* in February 1949 Arthur Miller published an essay in the *New York Times* entitled "Tragedy and the Common Man." The essay is clearly meant to provide the theoretical basis for what Miller aimed to achieve in writing the drama that has in the passing decades often been recognized as the embodiment of a literary subgenre designated as "modern" in contrast with "classical" tragedy. If Miller has accurately assessed the special character of what tragedy must mean in the context of "modernism" he has then both created a drama that diverges widely from Greek and Shakespearean concepts of the nature of tragedy and developed a theory, an alternate *Poetics,* that confronts and contradicts long held principles established by Aristotle in the *Poetics* for understanding the nature of this genre. I propose that *Death of a Salesman,* although failing the test for authenticity in Aristotelian terms, lays a plausible claim to the creation of an alternate "modern" literary genre that is of genuine cultural importance, whether or not we are prepared to accord it the traditional designation of "tragedy." Moreover, a serious question arises as to whether Willy Loman, the protagonist of Miller's drama, manifests or, in fact, contradicts, essential aspects of Miller's own theoretical requirements for the construction of a "modern" iteration of the genre we know as "classical tragedy." In this regard, the following relevant passages in Miller's essay explain the author's perspective:

> Generally, to which there may be exceptions unknown to me, I think the tragic feeling is evoked in us when we are in the presence of a character who is ready to lay down his life, if need be, to secure one thing—his sense of personal dignity. From Orestes to Hamlet, Medea to Macbeth, the underlying struggle is that of the individual attempting to gain his "rightful" position in his society.
>
> Sometimes he is one who has been displaced from it, sometimes one who seeks to attain it for the first time, but the fateful wound from which the inevitable events spiral is the wound of indignity, and its dominant force is indignation. Tragedy, then, is the consequence of a man's total compulsion to evaluate himself justly.[29]

> The possibility of victory must be there in tragedy. Where pathos rules, where pathos is finally derived, a character has fought a battle he could not possibly have won. The pathetic

is achieved when the protagonist is, by his witlessness, his insensitivity or the very air he gives off, incapable of grappling with a much superior force.

Pathos truly is the mode for the pessimist. But tragedy requires a nicer balance between what is possible and what is impossible. And it is curious, although edifying, that the plays we revere, century after century, are the tragedies. In them, and in them alone, lies the belief—optimistic, if you will, in the perfectibility of man.[30]

In discussing *Oedipus*, we benefited from the perceptive guidance of E. R. Dodds and in our analysis of *Othello*, A. C. Bradley's critical discernment was very useful to us. More numerous and diverse have been the commentaries on *Death of a Salesman*, but two essays written near the time of the first production of the play offer insights that I find are especially skillful in capturing what the play does and does not achieve:

The play [John Gassner writes] is not quite the masterpiece of dramatic literature that the enthusiasts would have us believe. It is well written, but is not sustained by incandescent or memorable language except in two or three short passages. Moreover, its hero, the desperate salesman Willy Loman, is too much the loud-mouthed dolt and emotional babe-in-the-woods to wear all the trappings of high tragedy with which he has been invested. For modern writers of the school of Molière and Shaw Willy would have been an object of satirical penetration rather than mournful tenderness and lachrymose elegy . . . .

Once these reservations are made, however, one cannot deny that the play has singular merits, that it is often moving and even gripping, that it is penetrative both in characterization and social implication. It expresses a viewpoint of considerable importance when it exposes the delusions of "go-getting," "contacts"—inebriated philistinism by reducing it to the muddle of Willy's life which is surely not an isolated case . . . . [The] interest and sympathy [of the audience] are engaged by the pathos of a man who gave all his life to a business only to be thrown on the scrap-heap . . . . an American *naïf* bemused by the worship of uncreative success and hollow assumptions that "personality" is the *summum bonum* . . . . My criticism that the play over valuates a vacuous individual requires this important qualification: Willy who is otherwise so unimpressive, is translated into a father for whom the love and success of his favorite son Biff is a paramount necessity and a consuming passion. He has been made into a dramatically charged father-hero, and as such becomes a heroic figure in active pursuit of the father-son ideal. He may be a fool, but he becomes a monolithic figure of some tragic dimension in this respect. [In] this man who is a failure even as a bourgeois . . . . Miller has created an intensification of humanity that lifts the drama above the level of the humdrum.[31]

[Willy's] misfortune [John Mason Brown writes] is that he has gone through life as an eternal adolescent, as someone who has not dared to take stock, as someone who never knew who he was. His personality has been his profession; his energy, his protection. His major ambition has been not only to be liked, but to be well liked. His ideal for himself and for his sons has stopped with an easy back-slapping, sports-loving, locker-room popularity. More than ruining his sons so that one has become a woman chaser and the other a thief, his standards have turned both boys against their father . . . . [Mr. Miller] writes boldly and brilliantly about the way in which we disappoint those we love by having disappointed ourselves. He knows the torment of family tensions, the compensations of friendship, and the heartbreak that goes with broken pride and lost confidence. He is aware of the loyalties, not blind, but open-eyed, which are needed to support mortals in their loneliness. The anatomy of failure, the pathos of age, and the tragedy of those years when a life begins to slip down the hill it has labored to climb are subjects at which he excels.[32]

There is an obvious, enormous challenge to contemporary readers and critics in Miller's attempt to declare in "Tragedy and the Common Man" that the field of tragedy is now as open from the twentieth century on for the common man, for someone like Willy Loman, to share the high tragic arena equally with the paradigmatic heroes of Greek and Shakespearean tragedy. I think that our inquiry into the disparity between the claim to tragic status of Oedipus and Othello in contrast with that of Willy Loman should be investigated first on the basis of Miller's assertion, cited earlier, that: "As a general rule, to which there may be exceptions unknown to me, I think that the tragic feeling is evoked in us when we are in the presence of a character who is ready to lay down his life, if need be, to secure one thing— his sense of personal dignity. From Orestes to Hamlet, Medea to Macbeth, the underlying struggle is that of the individual attempting to gain his 'rightful' place in his society."[33]

I think that there is no doubt that both Oedipus and Othello have been dislodged from the fate justly due to them based on their demonstrated virtues and good character by hostile external forces, either supernatural and inexplicable, on the one hand, or profoundly and unaccountably malevolent, on the other. Both Oedipus and Othello could validly urge in their favor that nothing in their character and actions earned them the destinies that befell them and so their efforts were legitimately focused on gaining their "rightful" place in society. If now with the guidance of Gassner and Brown, we ponder the character and actions of

Willy Loman from the beginning of *Death of a Salesman* to the end, I see no reason to extend an equal and parallel accolade to Willy. First and foremost, we note the moral and spiritual chasm that divides Oedipus and Othello from Willy Loman. The Greek and Shakespearean heroes completely differ from Willy in that they met their dooms after having risen to high plateaus of achievement and prosperity before falling into misery, which, we remember, is a major determinative circumstance for tragedy in Aristotle's *Poetics*. Of equal importance is the fact that the agency of their fall was external to their essential character, while the force propelling Willy to his ruin is an authentic tragic flaw deeply embedded, as we shall see, in his inner nature.

WILLY LOMAN AS TRAGIC HERO: THE QUESTION OF *HAMARTIA*

In his introduction to his *Collected Plays*, Arthur Miller confronts the issue which has troubled many critics of *Death of a Salesman*: the status of Willy Loman as a tragic hero in comparison with classical and Shakespearean representations of such a hero. It is with eloquence and passion that Miller defies the critics who deny Willy classical tragic status (and I will prove to be one of them) and advocates an anti-Aristotelian theory of tragedy that would make him a worthy partner of Oedipus and Othello in the phenomenon we recognize as the tragic concept of human existence. I cite below important passages of his introduction that justly inspire and require an Aristotelian response:

> The play was always heroic to me, and in later years the acad-
> emy's charge that Willy lacked the "stature" for the tragic
> hero seemed incredible to me . . . . I set out not to "write

a tragedy" in this play, but to show the truth as I saw it. However, some of the attacks upon it as a pseudo-tragedy contain ideas so misleading, and in some cases so laughable, that it might be in place here to deal with a few of them.

Aristotle, having spoken of a fall from the heights, it goes without saying that someone of the common mold cannot be a fit tragic hero. It is now many centuries since Aristotle lived. There is now no more reason for falling in a faint before his *Poetics* than before Euclid's geometry, which has been amended numerous times by men with new insights; nor, for that matter, would I choose to have my illnesses diagnosed by Hippocrates rather than the most ordinary graduate of an American medical school, despite the Greek's genius. Things do change, and even a genius is limited by his time and the nature of his society . . . . There is a legitimate question of stature here, but none of rank, which is so often confused with it. *So long as the hero may be said to have had alternatives of a magnitude to have materially changed the course of his life, it seems to me that in this respect at least, he cannot be debarred from the heroic role* (italics mine).

The question of rank is significant to me only as it reflects the question of the social application of the hero's career. There is no doubt that if a character is shown on the stage who goes through the most ordinary actions, and is suddenly revealed to be the President of the United States, his actions immediately assume a much greater magnitude, and pose the possibility of a much greater meaning, than if he is the corner grocer. But at the same time, his stature as a hero is not so utterly dependent upon his rank that the corner grocer cannot outdistance him as a tragic figure—providing, of course, that the grocer's career engages the issues of, for instance, the *survival of the race, the relationships of man to God—the questions, in short, whose answers define humanity and the right way to live* . . . . (italics mine)

It was not out of any deference to a definition that Willy

Loman is filled with a joy, however broken-hearted, as he approaches his end, but simply that my sense of his character dictated his joy, and even what I felt was an exultation. In terms of his character, he has achieved an important piece of knowledge, *which is that he is loved by his son and has been embraced by him and forgiven* (italics mine). In this he is given his existence, so to speak—his fatherhood, for which he has always striven and until now could not achieve. *That he is unable to take this victory thoroughly to his heart, that it closes the circle for him and propels him to his death, is the wage of his sin, which was to have committed himself so completely to the counterfeits of dignity and the false coinage embodied in his idea of success that he can prove his existence only by bestowing "power" on his posterity, a power deriving from the sale of his last asset, himself, for the price of his insurance policy* (italics mine).[34]

Here we now arrive at the point where we can put to a persuasive test the claim of ranking Willy Loman as a tragic hero in a class with Oedipus and Othello. The criteria Miller has given us for making such a judgment are whether Willy has endured in his life experiences such soaring challenges as probing the relationship of man to God and devotion to the scrutiny of such profound issues as those that define the essential nature of our humanity. Now Oedipus clearly ponders the possible role of divine intervention in the fate that befell him and questions harshly (and most would say unfairly) his personal responsibility as a human agent in the crimes he was led to commit. These were crimes that the world (his and ours) judge to be objectively horrific, but for which the world (his and ours) deem him to be subjectively innocent. Othello, in turn, deems Iago the diabolical force that drove him against his will to accuse, condemn, and take the life of an innocent Desdemona but cannot allow himself to survive the objectively horrific crime against his loyal lover for which the world (his and ours) would easily and gladly maintain that he is subjectively innocent. It is important to recognize that both Oedipus and Othello lay a claim to tragic heroism based on the dignity and courage which they demonstrate in enduring a responsibility for a fate that was thrust upon them by either an external divine or human agency that propelled them into objectively horrific destinies but for which their own inherent humanity *was totally innocent, was subjectively without guilt.* Miller himself recognizes that Willy Loman's situation is totally different from that of the classical tragic heroes.[35] He acknowledges that unlike Oedipus and Othello, who are devastated by external forces that overwhelm them, Willy's path to possible tragic heroism is blocked by internal psychological processes and character failures which we would have every right to expect a man to exert mastery over during a normal and ordinary human existence. Miller sees Willy seeking a tragic victory during the chaos and debacle of his life in finally achieving the dignity of a genuine father/son relationship in which he now has "a powerful piece of knowledge, which is that he is loved by his son and has been embraced by him and forgiven." When Miller charges Willy with suffering in the end from the "wage of his sin" in having committed himself "so completely to the counterfeits of dignity and the false coinage embodied in his idea of success," he removes him without equivocation from the ranks of genuine tragic heroes who have endured with dignity and strength the turmoil not of their own making assaulting the pillars of their existence. No one can accuse Oedipus or Othello of yielding to the "counterfeits of dignity" and "false coinage embodied in [an] idea of success." Their counter attack against the fates that unfairly assault them is driven by the authenticity of tragic heroism at its highest level.

DEATH OF A SALESMAN AND CATHARSIS

Words from *Oedipus Rex* and *Othello* guide us directly to the catharsis of *Death of a Salesman*:

> Nothing good comes from speaking of what should never have been done, so by the gods' will as quickly as possible hide me abroad or kill me or hurl me into the sea, where you shall never see me again. Come, consider it that it is right to touch a pitiful human being. Obey, do not be afraid. For except myself no one of mortals can bear my terrible fate
>
> (*Oedipus Tyrannos*, 1410–15).

> Speak of me as I am. Nothing extenuate,
> Nor set down aught in malice. Then you must speak
> Of one that loved not wisely but too well;
> Of one not easily jealous, but, being wrought
> Perplexed in the extreme; of one whose hand,
> Like the base Judean, threw a pearl away
> Richer than all his tribe; of one whose subdued eyes,
> Albeit unused to the melting mood,
> Drops tears as fast as the Arabian trees
> Their medicinable gum . . . .
> I kissed thee ere I killed thee. No way but this,
> Killing myself, to die upon a kiss.
> (He kisses Desdemona and dies).
>
> (*Othello*, 347–56, 364–65)

Biff: He had the wrong dreams. All, All, wrong.

Happy: almost ready to fight Biff: Don't say that!

Biff: He never knew who he was.

Charley: . . . . A Salesman has got to dream, boy. It comes with the territory.

Biff: Charley, the man didn't know who he was.

Happy, infuriated: Don't say that!

Biff: I know who I am, kid.

Happy: All right, boy. I'm going to show you and everybody else that Willy Loman did not die in vain. He had a good dream. It's the only dream you can have—to come out number-one man. He fought it out here, and this is where I'm gonna win it for him.

Biff, with a hopeless glance at Happy, bends toward his mother: Let's go Mom.

(Death of a Salesman, 138–39)

Biff's judgment on his father, "He never knew who he was," is a succinct summary of the illusions, delusions, and deceptions that Willy practiced upon himself and attempted to practice on those close to him to escape the recognition of his failure as a man, a father, and a husband. E. R. Dodds has given us a powerful and persuasive account of Oedipus's unflinching campaign to uncover the truth about his gloomy destiny, and Othello unhesitatingly pays a terrible price when he recognizes that a fate has befallen him far beyond any willful guilt on his part, but in compensation for which his agonized soul can accept no sacrifice less than the one that in the darkness of profound intellectual error he imposed on Desdemona. These classical tragic heroes endured objectively horrific destinies for which they were subjectively innocent. Above all, they behaved with integrity and courage in circumstances beyond their control. I don't think that it would be possible to argue that heroism was involved in any aspect of Willy's behavior or that in his numerous failures there were circumstances that he could not have overcome except for the weakness of his character.

If we catalog Willy's flaws, we can focus first on the illusions that he foists upon his sons that stir them to an undeserved and destructive form of hero worship of him. He fabricates stories of his popularity and success, which do not appear to have been fully justified in his best days as a salesman and bread winner and are completely without merit as he ages. He promotes superficial ideas such as the importance of being "well liked" over deeper and more enduring values, and encourages and praises Biff's initiative as a petty thief as an admirable characteristic. And this leads to greater failures in Biff's life as he commits at least one crime for which he serves jail time and then in his attempt to turn his life around when he returns home he steals a pen while waiting for an interview with the man who his shaky memory suggests once offered to be his patron when he worked for him years before. The purpose of the interview is to ask for a loan to start on a new road to success but in his long wait for the interview a clearer memory comes to the fore—the memory of his having stolen basketballs years earlier from the same man whose charity he is now seeking. The destructive influence of his father praising him for his initiative in stealing building materials comes back to haunt him here as he flees the office, the "patron," and the interview.

What credit can we give Willy for not taking a real job which Charley offers him instead of buttressing himself with the false pride of considering himself a superior human being to Charley because he will not subordinate himself to a man who has built a successful life but cannot put up a ceiling or build a porch for his house with, we recall, building materials stolen by his son whose "initiative" he has praised. (Willy to his sons: "Boys! Go right over there where they're building the apartment house and get some sand. We're going to rebuild the entire front stoop right now! . . . .

Biff: "Yes sir! On the double Hap!" [*Death of a Salesman*, 52]) Willy will not work for Charley but he will accept all the charity he can beg from him as he tries to hide his dark secret unsuccessfully from the world or at least certainly from Linda, his wife, who pities him for his humiliating behavior. Willy has no compunction about the crushing blow he is striking against Biff's self-worth and good character when he remarks to Linda and Charley with his own twisted pride "You shoulda seen the lumber they brought home last week at least a dozen six-by-tens worth all kinds of money." In a later conversation between Charley and Willy, Charley once again offers Willy a job which he refuses. (Willy: "I can't work for you, that's all, don't ask me why." Charley: "you been jealous of me all your life, you damned fool! Here, pay your insurance." He puts the money in Willy's hand [*Death of a Salesman*, 98].)

Biff is foolishly seduced by his father's warped vision of what constitutes success in the human condition, too easily lured into elevating Willy to a father/hero status because of his foolishly superabundant praise for a son, who views himself now as an adolescent hero slated for boundless success in the world. Burdened by an inflated ego because, in his father's words, he is "very well liked," and his petty thefts of building materials have already marked him out as someone capable of "courage and daring." Also more than one college has begun viewing him for his potential for athletic greatness. This proposed scenario falls apart, however, because Arthur Miller with sound artistic intuition (but perhaps not with full intentionality) smashes it to pieces by having Biff fail a math course that prevents his graduation. Biff, relying as always upon his father/hero for assistance, angry and disappointed, chases after him to Boston where he is on a sales trip. He is certain that someone in whom he believes as fervently as he believes in his father would be able to convince his teacher to give him the extra points that he needs to begin his great career as a college athlete. We will momentarily explain why Biff's mission fails, but a very important point needs to be made before that. In a conversation with Charley in his office Biff's boyhood friend, Bernard, now an adult and a successful lawyer, appears and Willy asks him why it was that Biff, right after he had followed Willy to Boston and then returned home, had completely abandoned his aspiration for a college career and the athletic stardom for which he had longed so passionately. Bernard thinks back to that critical time and says, "I've often thought of how strange it was that I knew [at that very moment] he'd given up his life" (*Death of a Salesman*, 94). What happened in Boston, Willy? What happened in Boston was, indeed, the death of a boy's spirit and the pathetic triumph of a father's insipid, deluded, and ruinous dreams.

For the purpose of telling this story Miller then skillfully interlaces two incidents that map out the disastrous course the drama of *Death of a Salesman* takes. The first stage of this disaster occurs when Biff and Happy seek to cheer up the despondent Willy with some good news. Biff tells Willy that he is going to see a former employer of his, Bill Oliver, whom he claims to Willy "always said, he'd stake me. I'd like to go into business so maybe I can take him up on it" (*Death of a Salesman*, 62). Biff, Happy, and Willy work up some unrealistic enthusiasm for this project and Biff claims that Oliver "did like me. Always liked me" (*Death of a Salesman*, 64). The reality of the meeting between Biff and Bill Oliver turns out be a parody of the great business deal imagined by Biff, Happy, and Willy. Biff tells Happy he waited all day (six hours) to see Oliver who exited his office at 5 o'clock and "didn't remember who I was or anything" (*Death of a Salesman*, 104). Then Biff says,

> he walked away. I saw him for one minute . . . . How the hell did I ever get the idea I was a salesman there? I even believed

myself that I'd been a salesman for him! And then he gave me one look and—I realized what a ridiculous lie my whole life has been. We've been talking in a dream for fifteen years. I was a shipping clerk . . . . The next thing I know I'm in his office . . . . I can't explain it . . . . I took his fountain pen . . . . I ran out. I ran down all eleven flights. I ran and ran and ran. (Biff at the table holding up a gold fountain pen, to Willy) so I am washed up with Oliver, you understand? Are you listening to me? I'm no good, can't you see what I am . . . . (Biff to Willy) We never told the truth for ten minutes in this house . . . . Now hear this Willy, this is me . . . . You know why I had no address for three months? I stole a suit in Kansas City and I was in jail . . . . I stole myself out of every good job since high school! . . . . And I never got anywhere because you blew me so full of hot air I could never stand taking orders from anybody . . . . It's goddam time you heard that.! I had to be boss big shot in two weeks, and I'm through with it . . . . I am not a leader of men, Willy, and neither are you. You were never anything but a hard-working drummer who landed in the ash can like the rest of them! I'm one dollar an hour, Willy! I tried seven states and couldn't raise it. A buck an hour! Do you gather my meaning? . . . . Pop, I'm nothing! I'm nothing, Pop. Can't you understand that?" (*Death of a Salesman*, 104)

The passages above represent one of two climactic points in act 2 of the play. They constitute one half of the "truth telling" core of the drama as they persuasively begin the process of creating the impassable chasm separating the heroes of classical tragedy and the protagonists of so many modern incarnations of the genre.

The second climactic point of the play occurs with the searing emotional crisis that assaults Biff when he locates his father in Boston and finds him sharing a room with a woman whose sexual favors have been purchased with stockings: (the woman:

"Where's my stockings? You promised me stockings, Willy! . . . . You had two boxes of size nine sheers for me, and I want them!" [*Death of a Salesman*, 119]) This conversation and Willy's desperate effort to drive the woman out of his room amid clumsy, fumbling attempts to explain to Biff her presence there, take place in front of a son suffering from delusional hero worship of a father. Biff's adoration of Willy has brought him to a Boston hotel room in the certain assurance that his "charismatic and well-liked" father will protect him against the failing grade in school that now threatens to block his path to a college scholarship and athletic stardom. As he witnesses the shredding of his father's reputation before his eyes he recognizes the illusions that are and have been Willy's stock in trade and squarely faces the grotesque charade that has been so far the life of the Loman family. It is now that Biff faces directly his father's infidelity to his long-suffering mother and betrayal of his family (remember the images in the play of his mother darning socks as his father, refusing the offer of honest employment, begs money from Charley to pay his bills). Traumatic events in his life also come into focus now: jail time in Kansas City for stealing a suit; much earlier, stealing building materials for his father (who proudly tells Charley that he can't control the "two fearless characters" he has been raising as his sons) and also the stolen basketballs from his employer, Bill Oliver, who may have been on the verge of firing him; and the final catastrophe, he, an adult returning home as a failure, stealing Bill Oliver's gold fountain pen when on a mission to borrow money from him so as to start out on a new life of "success and high achievement."

Biff's rebellion against his father is a knife in the heart of Willy who is a serial exploiter of false illusions, but none of his lies and misrepresentations torment him more than the realization that he has betrayed the son he loved. One truth that Willy cannot evade, hard as he tries to conceal it, is that he bears the responsibility for the aimless wandering of his son over the trackless desert of his unraveling existence.

Both E. R. Dodds and A. C. Bradley were able to call our attention to ennobling moments in the denouement that unfolds in both *Oedipus Rex* and *Othello*. The climax of *Death of a Salesman* is resonant with the dark clouds of human failure. In an imaginary conversation with his brother Ben, Willy raises the possibility of winning back Biff's love by committing suicide and leaving the proceeds of his life insurance policy ($20,000) to his family. Ben makes a series of rational objections to this plan but in his dark desperation Willy has nothing else to lean on for support. Besides, he imagines that his funeral will be a magnificent event with crowds of Willy's old friends and admirers gathering to pay homage to him so Biff will finally know how great a man he was. This is another of Willy's failed illusions, for Linda comments on the funeral, "Why didn't anyone come?" The truth that emerges in this drama, not of high tragedy, but of pathos, is spoken twice, once by Willy when he justifies to Ben his plan for suicide by saying, "Does it take more guts to stand here the rest of my life ringing up a zero?" (*Death of a Salesman*, 126) And it is reinforced by Biff when he offers a fitting epitaph for Willy in the final *Requiem* scene of the play "he had the wrong dreams. All, all wrong . . . . He never knew who he was" (*Death of a Salesman*, 138).

V

CATHARSIS: THE KEY TO TRAGEDY, ANCIENT AND MODERN

The long, complex, unsettled history of the interpretation of *catharsis* in Aristotle's *Poetics* can be said to have achieved three major interpretive milestones over the past centuries: the purification theory, the purgation theory, and the intellectual clarification theory. It must be said that Jacob Bernays's identification of the term with the process of medical purgation, which was first published in 1857,[36] continues to dominate discussions of this concept. However, I believe that it can be demonstrated that the purgation theory violates not only basic canons of Aristotelian thought, but also some of the most profound insights about the nature of literary experience that have been offered by astute critics over the ages. In the following citations D. W. Lucas recognizes the basis of all three of the interpretive milestones mentioned above without himself accepting anyone of them as definitive:

> (1) [purgation theory] With the growth of medical science in the fifth century the word [Gk. *kathairo, katharsis*] came naturally to be applied to the removal or evacuation of morbid substances from the human system . . . . (2) [purification theory] *Katharsis,* rendered 'purification,' is a word with a strong suggestion of uplift, and the earlier commentators were content to take the sentence as meaning that tragedy was morally improving . . . . [and quoting Dr. Johnson] 'The passions are the great movers of human actions; but they are mixed with such impurities that it is necessary they should be purged or refined by means of terrour and pity' . . . . (3) [intellectual clarification theory] On [such a] foundation might be raised a theory of tragedy which would be acceptable to many; pity and fear are cleansed of their pain because the tragic situation is made comprehensible (Aristotle's pleasure in learning . . . .) and the poet's philosophic insight leads to a calm and passionless, or acquiescent, contemplation of the human condition.[37]

In his discussion linking catharsis with "purgation" and "purification," Lucas makes a connection with the many other critics and scholars, past and present, who have adopted these two widely recognized and competing views that in one form or another have dominated the debate about the meaning of this concept. The striking point about Lucas's summary is that he also recognizes a cognitive, intellectual dimension for the concept of catharsis that has only too rarely engaged our attention in the catharsis debate. To my knowledge, the argument that catharsis as used by Aristotle in the *Poetics* is best understood as "intellectual clarification" first appeared in the early twentieth century and lay dormant until in the middle and later parts of that century. It then assumed a dynamic momentum that signaled a paradigm shift among interpretive approaches to the problem of understanding Aristotle's concept of catharsis in the *Poetics*.

We may trace the introduction of this understanding of catharsis as intellectual clarification to two works published by S. O. Haupt (1911 and 1915). In these seminal publications on the subject, Haupt noted that he had once received a letter in 1907 from Otto Immisch a professor at the University of Giessen who discussed a number of topics in the *Poetics* and said that he reached the conclusion that catharsis "in Aristotle's sense was neither ethical nor hedonistic nor therapeutic but 'intellectual.'"[38] Haupt writes that he had struggled against Immisch's suggestion for a long time but finally had come to see the correctness of Immisch's view and that the interpretation of catharsis as " intellectual clarification" (*Aufklärung*) was the only appropriate one (*die einzig passende*) for the term as used in the *Poetics*. From the time of Haupt's contributions to the debate about catharsis in the early twentieth century to 1962, when I wrote my first article on the subject,[39] I found no major attempt to interpret catharsis in the *Poetics* as "intellectual clarification." The arguments used by Haupt to support his view of catharsis as "Aufklärung" ("intellectual clarification") lit no interpretive fires within the community of classical scholars, who then and now have either obediently followed the hallowed traditions that were forged by the concepts of "purgation" and "purification," or sometimes by new hybrid forms of the two, or still later by newer hypotheses that unfortunately, after a suitable lapse of time, have failed to radically change the landscape of catharsis interpretation.

Are we then doomed to never reach an unequivocal understanding of what Aristotle really meant by catharsis as a central concept in the *Poetics and consequently the key experience of literary interpretation for mankind?* I think that we must as vigorously as possible resist such a depressing conclusion and I shall now attempt to muster the relevant arguments that will enable us to avoid it. I urge that a firm, unambiguous solution to the catharsis question has been available to us if only we unify into a single persuasive argument an accumulation of powerful, interconnected insights from various twentieth-century sources.

First, we need to confront the error into which Bernays led us initially (in 1857) when he argued that the key to Aristotle's use of the term catharsis in the *Poetics* was the way in which that same term was used in the *Politics*. About that latter use, I have written elsewhere:

> The solution to the problem of *katharsis* comes from seeing that it is not a concept with a single meaning, but one with several clearly distinct significations. Aristotle made use of a medical connotation at *Politics* 1341 b 38–1342 a 11 where he draws on the purgation therapy of the Hippocratic physicians for the concept of homeopathic cure of excessive emotion by use of orgiastic melodies. This cure leaves the previously distressed sufferers in a state of relief "as if they had received medical treatment and *katharsis*." [Contrary to this specific medical usage of *katharsis* in the *Politics* passage above we have in the *Poetics*] "a tightly woven argument" in which Aristotle locates the roots, goal, and essential pleasure of all *mimesis* in the act of learning and inference (μανθάνειν καὶ συλλογίζεσθαι [*manthanein kai syllogizesthai*]), [and] recognizes the philosophical capacity of *mimesis* to lead us from the particular to the universal . . . .
>
> In this context medical purgation is an intrusive, alien idea with links to nothing else in the *Poetics*. But when in its place we have recourse to *katharsis* as a key term in the philosophical tradition whose roots are in Plato's *Sophist*, the situation changes radically. The *katharsis* of that philosophical tradi-

tion—*katharsis* as "intellectual clarification"—establishes a meaningful and organic relationship between key passages of the *Poetics* cited above (as in chapters 4, 9, and 14) and the definition of the *essence* of tragedy (chapter 6).[40]

In the *Sophist* 230d–e the Stranger says to Theaetetus that *elenchos*, the Socratic method of "cross-examination," that is of asking questions and refuting answers until agreement in a dispute is approached or reached and false opinion is demolished and replaced by the acceptance of a persuasive truth, is "the greatest and most authoritative of [all] forms of *katharsis*" (μεγίστη καὶ κυριωτάτη τῶν καθάρσεών ἐστι; Gk. *megistē kai kuriotatē tōn katharseōn esti*). This cognitive catharsis does make a significant connection with other cognitive terms and judgments in the *Poetics*. Thus there is the phrase in chapter 4 that "learning is not only most pleasant for philosophers but for others similarly, only they share in it to a lesser degree because they enjoy viewing images since in contemplating them *it turns out that they learn and infer* (Gk. *manthanein kai syllogizesthai*—italics mine) what each thing is"; the statement in chapter 9 that poetry "is more philosophical and more significant than history"; and the description of the elements, essence, and purpose of tragedy in chapter 6.

In rejecting Bernays's linkage of the use of catharsis in the *Politics* with its use in the *Poetics*, we should keep in mind the following admonition of Richard McKeon:

> To cite what is said concerning art in the *Politics* in refutation or in expansion of what is said on the same subject in the *Poetics*, without recognizing that the one is a political utterance, the other an aesthetic utterance, would be an error comparable to looking for evolution or refutation between

the statements of the *Republic* and the *Laws,* without recognizing that the one has reference to a perfect state, the other to a state possible to men as they are.[41]

We are now able to move on from what catharsis in the *Poetics is not* and what there is a very great likelihood that it *must be.* I have called attention earlier to the fact that Plato in the *Sophist* (230d–e) had described *elenchos*, the Socratic process of "cross-examination," in a philosophical debate to move from ignorance to knowledge as the "greatest and most authoritative of all forms of *katharsis.*" In her important study *The Fragility of Goodness,* Martha Nussbaum endorses and significantly expands the close link that I assert exists between catharsis as a cognitive term in the *Poetics* and the large number of words derived from the *kathar-* root, which are used in the Greek philosophical and rhetorical vocabularies that have related cognitive significance. Nussbaum writes:

> Golden points out that if we look to Plato's epistemological vocabulary . . . . we find in fact that *katharsis* and related words especially in the middle dialogues, have a strong connection with learning . . . . We can, however, press this point much harder than Golden did if we look briefly at the whole history of *katharsis* and related words (*kathairo, katharos,* etc.). These facts are straightforward and easily accessible; they need to be stated, however, since they have too often been forgotten in discussions of this topic. When we examine the whole range of use and development of this word-family, it becomes quite evident that the primary, ongoing, central meaning is roughly one of "clearing up" or "clarification" . . . . If we now return to Plato's usage, we find that he preserves this general picture . . . . *Katharos* cognition is what we have when the soul is not impeded by bodily obstacles (esp. *Rep.* 508C,

Phd. 69C . . . . the *katharon* becomes associated with the true or truly knowable, the being who has achieved *katharsis* with the truly or correctly knowing (esp. *Phd.* 65ff., 110ff.). Thus, we even find expressions such as *katharōs apodeixai* meaning "demonstrate clearly" (*Crat.* 426B). We can now add that by Aristotle's time and shortly thereafter—whether through Plato's influence or through an independent development of the applications to speech—this epistemological use of *katharsis* and *katharos* becomes easy and natural, and does not even require a context of metaphor. Xenophon speaks of a *katharos nous*, meaning one that cognizes clearly and truly (*Cyr.* 8.7.30). Epicurus speaks . . . . of a *katharsis phusikōn problematōn*, a clarification of the difficult issues of natural philosophy . . . . *kathairo* means "explain" [and] Aristotle's *Prior Analytics* speaks of a need to examine and indicate each of these things with clarity (*katharōs*) (50a40); it goes without saying that these uses have nothing to do either with purification or with purgation.[42]

We have seen that there are compelling reasons on the basis of the philological evidence for the way catharsis and its family of words are used in Greek philosophical and epistemological contexts for assigning the meaning of "intellectual clarification" to the term in the much debated context in which it appears in the *Poetics*. Thus, philological probability contributes emphatic, decisive evidence for defining catharsis in the *Poetics* as "clarification" or "illumination." But of even greater weight than philological probability is the fact that catharsis is the element that imposes upon a work of art its essential structural integrity. In achieving artistic distinction at the highest level, catharsis supplies art work its impregnable foundation, which binds that entire work together as a persuasive, meaningful unity. It is thus the determining factor of whether, and to what degree, a work of art fulfills its destiny. Now, what is its destiny? Highest ranking among many possible values I suggest that it is to continually endure probing inquiry into its meaning by mankind, to long maintain an untarnished reputation for relevance and importance for humanity, and most importantly, to make the complexity of the human condition comprehensible to all who seek a means to dissipate the choking fog of their existential confusion. Literature among all the arts contains the massive, flexible infrastructure of techniques and skills that can support a platform of electrifying epiphanies and brilliant illuminations. Catharsis (intellectual clarification) represents the sum of these epiphanies and illuminations that is our fortunate heritage from the many peerless artistic achievements of the long history of our civilization. Three chapters of the *Poetics*—4, 6, and 9—make an essential contribution to the cognitive interpretation of catharsis. We begin with chapter 4 (1448b4-b17):

> Speaking generally, the origin of the art of poetry is to be found in two natural causes. For the process of imitation is natural to mankind from childhood on. Man is differentiated from other animals because he is the most imitative of them, and he learns his first lessons through imitation, and we observe that all men find pleasure in imitations. The proof of this is what happens in life. For there are some things that distress us when we see them but the most accurate representations of these same things we view with pleasure—as, for example, the forms of the most despised animals and of corpses. The cause of this is that *the act of learning is not only most pleasant to philosophers but, in a similar way, to other men as well, only they have an abbreviated share in this pleasure. Thus, men find pleasure in viewing representations because it turns out that they learn and infer what each thing is—for example, that this object is that kind of object* (italics mine).

In his commentary on the *Poetics* O. B. Hardison, Jr., explains the essential importance of this passage:

> The pleasure derived from imitative works is not sense-gratification but a type of pleasure associated with learning. This learning, in turn comes from observing "that this particular object is that kind of object . . . . According to Aristotle (for example, *Metaphysics,* 1036a28, 1059b29), "learning occurs when we come to know universals or perceive the relationship of the specific to the universal . . . . It is a key concept, for it emphatically differentiates Aristotle's "imitation" from the Platonic notion of imitation as copying . . . . he is referring to the fact that imitative works, if they are well done, reveal generic qualities—the presence of the universal in the particular—and that the spectator or audience learns because of this . . . . [For example,] Even if we have never been to the seashore we can learn a great deal about the seagull from looking at Audubon's illustration [of one]. At the same time, as everyone knows, Audubon's paintings are works of art. They give pleasure and the source of the pleasure according to Aristotle is their communication of the universal in the particular. This point is central to Aristotle's theory of art.[43]

Hardison argues with unmistakable clarity that in this chapter Aristotle asserts his basic principle about literary works of art. Namely, the goal of a work of art is to represent a skillfully organized series of characters and actions that is set in the framework of the play's developing plot. These events have the structural potency to evoke for an audience the universal causal principles that drive those actions and characters and make them persuasively understandable in terms of the laws of nature and human behavior. That is, in a great work of art the climactic sensation will be an important cognitive experience, a catharsis, which will raise the audience's attention from the particulars on the stage or page to a comprehension of fundamental laws governing the human condition. That act of cognitive insight represents, for Aristotle, the quintessential pleasure of all aesthetic responses although many other subordinate pleasures are embedded in works of art. Thus if we read *Oedipus Rex*, *Othello*, and *Death of a Salesman* in depth, paying attention to the witness they bear about the experience of being human, we will be rewarded with more than some kind of superficial pleasures related to diction and spectacle (although there will not be any scarcity of these). More than that, on a general level we will be induced into a confrontation with the reality of our own existences. Whatever there is in our reality—experiences of pain and pleasure, of heroism and cowardice, of truth and falsity—will be transformed into a permanent store of wisdom for us. This enrichment then becomes a priceless enhancement of our humanity, a catharsis more triumphant and rewarding than any other response to tragedy could be.

Secondly, it is in chapter 6 of the *Poetics* that the intellectually and emotionally charged term catharsis appears for the first and only time as the climactic goal of tragic experience. Here is that definitive passage (1449b21–28):

> We shall speak about the form of imitation that is associated with hexameter verse and comedy later. Let us now discuss tragedy, bringing together the definition of its essence that has emerged from what we have already said. Tragedy is, then, an imitation of a noble and complete action, having the proper magnitude; it employs language that has been artistically enhanced by each of the kinds of linguistic adornment, applied separately in the various parts of the play; it is presented in dramatic, not narrative form, and

achieves, through the representation of pitiable and fearful incidents, the *catharsis* [Gk. κάθαρσιν] of such pitiable and fearful incidents.[44]

Professor Hardison comments with lucidity and persuasively on this important statement:

> To understand what "*katharsis* of incidents arousing pity and fear" means we need to recall two points. First, the Greek word *katharsis can* mean "clarification" as well as "purgation" or "purification." Second, in chapter 4 Aristotle at some length insists that imitation does not produce "pleasure in general" but only the kind of pleasure that comes from learning. He further states this learning comes from discovering a relation between the object represented and certain universal elements embodied in it . . . . The tragic poet begins by selecting a series of incidents that are intrinsically pitiable or fearful . . . . He then presents them in such a way as to bring out the probable or necessary principles that unite them in a single action and determine their relation to this action as it proceeds from beginning to the end. When the spectator has witnessed a tragedy of this type, he will have learned something—the incidents will be clarified in the sense that their relation in terms of universals will have become manifest— and the act of learning, says Aristotle, will be enjoyable. This interpretation of the catharsis clause in chapter 6 [was the subject of a series of studies by Leon Golden in the mid and late 20th century]. It has many virtues. In the first place, it makes the clause a reference to the *techne* of tragedy, not to the psychology of the audience. Second, it relates katharsis *both* to the theory of imitation outlined in chapters 1–4 and to the discussion of probability and necessity in chapter 9. Moreover, it coincides with much current aesthetic theory. This is not to say that the "clarification theory" of catharsis is

right because it makes Aristotle agree with modern writers, but rather to say that Aristotle and modern aestheticians both attempt to define the same thing and one need not be surprised to find parallels in their conclusions. The modern aesthetician might say that a work of art is successful in so far as it achieves "coherence" and that the discovery of this "coherence" is the essential aesthetic pleasure. Francis Ferguson considers "perception" the third and climactic stage of both tragic action and of the audience's experience; James Joyce uses the term "epiphany" (a vision of truth) to describe the effect created when a series of apparently disparate events suddenly assume coherence in the mind; and Austin Warren uses the phrase "rage for order" to describe both the object of the poet's quest and the need in the reader that is satisfied by poetry. What these critics have in mind is what depth psychology calls an "insight experience." Aristotle's comments in chapters 4, 6, and 9 indicate that he considered the experience of tragedy a kind of "insight experience": (1) the experience is pleasurable, not painful as the same events would be if experienced in "real life"; (2) the pleasure is the kind that results from learning; (3) the learning is related to the discovery of the relation between the particulars of the plot *via* the universals that make the particulars coherent; and (4) the term designating the tragic function is *katharsis*—something like "clarification."[45]

Chapter 9 is the third relevant chapter in this context. I cite lines 1451a37 to 1451b11 below and then follow with Professor Hardison's commentary:

It is apparent from what we have said that it is not the function of the poet to narrate events that have actually happened, but, rather, events such as might occur and have the capability of occurring in accordance with the laws of probability or necessity. For the historian and the poet do not differ by their writing in prose or verse (the works of Herodotus might be put into verse but they would, nonetheless, remain a form of history both in their metrical and prose versions.) The difference, rather, lies in the fact that the historian narrates events that have actually happened, whereas the poet writes about things as they might possibly occur. Poetry, therefore, is more philosophical and more significant than history, for poetry is more concerned with the universal and history more with the individual. By the universal I mean what sort of a man turns out to say or do what sort of thing according to probability or necessity—this being the goal poetry aims at, although it gives individual names to the characters whose actions are imitated. By the individual I mean a statement telling, for example, "what Alcibiades did or experienced."

Professor Hardison makes the following comments on chapter 9:

Chapter 9 is especially rich in fundamental ideas about art. Logically, it moves from the discussion of unity as a general concept to a discussion of the general qualities that relate the incidents in a well-ordered plot. These are probability (*eikos*) and necessity (*ananke*). They are present in poetry, Aristotle says, but not (or not normally) in history. Their presence justifies the statement that poetry is "more philosophical" than history and that its statements are "more concerned with the universal" . . . . What does Aristotle mean by "necessity or probability?" The most obvious answer to the question is that necessity and probability are principles of causality . . . . Among other things, this line of thought explains why Aristotle regularly uses not one but both terms when discussing tragic plots. Necessity is not merely a "more rigorous" kind of probability, it is something quite different. An

event that is "necessary" is not probable and vice versa . . . .
we can understand probability and necessity simply as
those unifying principles brought out by the arrangement
of the incidents . . . . If a drama has unity, it has necessity
or probability . . . . We . . . . have two kinds of causality
operating in dramatic plots—the general one in which the
unifying principle "causes" all the incidents in the play; and
the more specific one in which episode 2 is the direct cause
of episode 3.[46]

We now come to the concluding phase of our investigation
in which we review four strong pillars of justification for ranking
"intellectual clarification" as the demonstrable interpretation of
choice (over purgation, purification, and all other competitors)
concerning the precise meaning of catharsis. The long and so far
fruitless search to establish its meaning univocally, persuasively,
and with finality, turns on the long disputed, provocative phrase
in chapter 6 of the *Poetics* that tragedy "achieves through the
representation (*mimesis*) of pitiable and fearful incidents the
katharsis of such pitiable and fearful incidents." These four pillars are (1) the philological evidence, (2) evidence from the core
argument of the *Poetics*, (3) evidence from a psychoanalytical
perspective, and (4) the judgment of a distinguished practicing
drama critic of the last century.

PHILOLOGICAL EVIDENCE FOR CATHARSIS AS "INTELLECTUAL CLARIFICATION"

1. Plato, *Sophist, 230*d–e. The statement is made that the
   Socratic process of *elenchos* (the question–and–answer
   "cross examination" of clashing arguments in a philosophi-

cal debate that leads to a continuing refinement in the truth value achieved in that argument) is "the greatest and most authoritative of all forms of *katharsis.*" This Platonic application of the term catharsis is a powerful, perhaps the most powerful, witness we have outside the *Poetics*, to the capacity of this term to express a cognitive theme of immense importance in a philosophical context.

2. The comprehensive collection of examples cited in the foregoing section by Professor Martha Nussbaum, which described the range of meanings of the entire *kathar*-family of words used in prominent cognitive contexts. She adds to her analysis of the *kathar*-root words the following:

> the central sense is that of freedom from admixture, clarity, absence of impediment. In the case of the soul and its cognition, the application of the word-group is mediated by the dominant metaphors of mud and clean light: the eye of the soul can be sunk in mud . . . . or it can be seeing cleanly and clearly. *Katharos cognition* is what we have when the soul is not impeded by bodily obstacles . . . . *Katharsis* is the clearing up of the vision of the soul by the removal of these obstacles; thus, the *katharon* becomes associated with the true or truly knowable, the being who has achieved *katharsis with* the truly or correctly knowing . . . . Thus, we even find expressions such as *katharos apodeixis.* meaning "demonstrate clearly."[47]

FROM MIMESIS TO CATHARSIS: THE CORE ARGUMENT OF THE *POETICS*

In this section I plan to deal with concepts which appear in various chapters of the *Poetics* and which serve as structural elements in supporting the argument for interpreting catharsis as "intellectual clarification." I begin first with mimesis. In chapter 1 Aristotle comments that the many literary and musical arts invented by mankind are, viewed collectively, forms of mimesis directed at the range of human actions and behavior. Elsewhere I have described Aristotle's concept of mimesis in a way that shows the close connection it has with catharsis understood as "intellectual clarification":

> For Aristotle, *mimesis* is a tightly structured process involving, in different arts, different means of representation, different manners of communicating that representation to an audience, and different moral and ethical states as the object of artistic representation. Thus, some arts use words, rhythm and harmony, and others color and form to communicate to an audience, some arts require a stage and actors for their presentation and others only a single narrator; and some arts represent noble, and others ignoble, characters and actions. All forms of *mimesis,* however, have a common origin in "mankind's desire to know," a common means of satisfying that desire by leading us to perceive the universal principles inherent in the particulars of every significant work of art. They provide a common pleasure—the intellectual pleasure of "learning and inference" (*manthanein kai sullogizesthai)—* which is the highest human pleasure.[48]

Aristotle forges an unbreakable link between mimesis and catharsis by asserting in chapter 4 that it is by mimesis that we human beings are uniquely led to achieving the cognitive pleasure (catharsis) innate to our status as the most imitative of all creatures in the universe: it being granted to us alone to master by "learning and inference" the facts of the world of reality by relating the particulars of individual events to the universal causal principles that clarify and explain them. Neither "purgation" nor "purification" nor any other suggested interpretation of catharsis has the power or relevance to create this unity between the key terms in chapters 4 and 6 in the *Poetics*. D. W. Lucas, without making an explicit link to catharsis, adds further substance to the argument that I have been making as follows:

> Where Aristotle showed his originality was in stressing the element of structure . . . . Here it is important how far Plato and Aristotle followed the same path, and where Aristotle went beyond Plato. Plato asserted in the *Phaedrus* (268 D) that a tragedy (a representation of men in action, *Rep.* 603 C) was not a mere sequence of speeches but a structure so ordered that the parts stood in proper relation to each other and the whole. The meaning of this can be filled out from the criticism of Lysias' speech given shortly before (264 B–E), where in terms similar to those used by Aristotle in Chapters 7 and 8 it is laid down that the parts must be "organically" connected as in an animal, so forming a whole, single and complete. Where Aristotle goes beyond Plato is extending to a mimetic form the conception of a causally united structure. Structure in a speech gives intellectual satisfaction because the parts are logically related and proportioned, and no doubt aesthetic satisfaction as well. But a play, the imitation of an action, if its parts are in a necessary causal relationship with each other and the whole, reveals something about the nature of an action under the conditions obtaining in our world. This is the point reached in the first climax of the *Poetics* in Ch. 9. It is because a properly constructed plot shows a general truth about the sort of thing that is done by certain sorts of men that poetry is, in the famous phrase (51b5), "more important and more philosophical than history," a universally valid representation of life. J. H.

Newman in his youthful *Essay on Poetry* put the essence of the matter in a way that has not been bettered: "by confining the attention to one series of events and scene of action, it (tragedy) bounds and finishes off the confused luxuriance of real nature; while by a skillful adjustment of circumstances, it brings into sight the connection between cause and effect, completes the dependence of the parts one on another, and harmonizes the proportions of the whole."[49]

Lucas correctly observes Aristotle's requirement that the action in a tragedy must represent a "causally united structure." This is of the utmost importance because only such a "causally united structure" can link itself to the key theme in chapter 4 of mimesis as the instrument of the pleasure uniquely achieved by humanity in the act of "learning and inference." This linkage takes place because only a "causally united structure" can make the action represented in a mimetic representation intellectually credible and therefore available for assessment cognitively. And, of course, a cognitive assessment is required if the "learning and inference" is to take place, which is the function attributed to mimesis in the *Poetics*. In this connection, we should recall that in chapter 9 Aristotle sets down the requirement that the tragic plot represented in a dramatic mimesis must be controlled by the forces of *necessity or probability*. Now it must be clear that the "causally united structure" required by Aristotle in mimetic representations is such *only because* it is under control of the principles of *necessity or probability* as described in chapter 9. It also should become clear that a plot with a "causally united structure" under control of the principles of *necessity or probability* can only make a viable connection with the stated goal of artistic mimesis in chapter 6, that is catharsis, if that much-debated concept is understood as generating the "learning and inference" that is the basis of cognitive pleasure, and thus that it (catharsis) signifies "intellectual clarification." Thus, I argue, it becomes inevitable that we must reject the impulse to link catharsis to "purgation" or "purification" since those concepts (as well as, apparently, all others that have been suggested) totally fail the test of relevancy to the climactic cognitive experience of the "causally united structure governed by necessity or probability." The events of *Oedipus Rex, Othello,* and *Death of a Salesman* are riveting and persuasive because we are convinced that necessary or probable forces (not irrational, aimless chance) are controlling the events that are unfolding in these mimetic representations and so leading meaningfully to deep learning and understanding about the human condition. That intimate and valuable connection between ourselves as human beings and the work of art is not made if we have recourse to interpretations of catharsis that bear no cognitive connection to the imitative pleasure that is a defining element of our humanity and, it can be argued, the very purpose of our being human.

A PSYCHOANALYTICAL PERSPECTIVE

Professor Bennett Simon, Harvard psychiatrist and perceptive commentator on the linkage between psychoanalysis and Greek tragedy offers the following valuable insights:

> There is a confluence, then, between these views of what Aristotle is saying about the art of tragedy and what contemporary ego psychology says about the nature of psychoanalysis and the complex ways it effects its cure. The views of such classicists as Gerald Else and Leon Golden can be termed ego-psychological approaches to Aristotle . . . . With these

considerations at hand, we can now move the discussion of theater as therapy into a different framework, that of the similarities of what one derives from drama and what one derives from psychoanalytic insight . . . . Both therapy and theater should give an enhanced awareness of the tragic dimension of human life . . . . Affects and emotions become more refined, more differentiated, and in a way more discriminating. Pity and terror are not purged but transmuted and integrated into a new level of response and understanding. In this respect, I believe that Aristotle's notion of catharsis has been misunderstood to mean a primitive kind of purging. The Oedipus plays of Sophocles illustrate the movement from primitive dread of pollution because of unspeakable deeds to a more refined and focused sense of moral responsibility. Terror and madness are not made to disappear; they are refined and integrated in the dramatic resolutions . . . . Related to the change in the experience of emotions is a reshuffling and reintegration of thoughts and emotions. "Tragic knowledge" implies that by the end of the play the characters and the audience know things they did not know before, and know them in a way they have not experienced before. If we consider Aristotle's notion of the pleasure tragedy provides, we find that a scale of pleasures is implied. The pleasure of tragedy is of a higher order than the more undifferentiated desires and lusts of humankind. Tragedy, too, must in some ways stir up the body as well as the soul; but Aristotle's views of the highest forms of pleasure, including that of tragedy, assume an increasing differentiation of the bodily appetites and responses along with more discriminating cognitive responses. One is thrilled by a well-constructed play, but decidedly not in the same way one may shudder at an unadorned scene of terror, destruction, or sexuality . . . . Finally, tragedy should bring some altered and new sense of what one is and who he is in relation to those around him. The tragic figures in the plays struggle with their relationships and obligations to those in their past, present, and future.

The audience acquires a new sense of the possibilities in being human and in coming to terms with the forces that are more powerful than any one individual. In therapy, we also expect an enlarged view of the possibilities that are open in relationships to the self and to others. Thus, good therapy and good theater have in common a set of inner processes. Theater is not, and was not for the Greeks, primarily intended to be therapy for especially disturbed or distressed people. It was expected to provide a certain form of pleasure, even in Greek culture, and was an integral part of the *paideia* (education in the broadest sense) of each Athenian.[50]

THE JUDGMENT OF A PRACTICING DRAMA CRITIC

John Gassner, in his oft-cited 1937 article "Catharsis and the Modern Theater," speaks to the role of catharsis in drama criticism:

> Has it not always been recognized that the superiority of the great tragedies, if we exclude purely stylistic differences, has resided in their powerful blending of passion with enlightenment? This is what we mean when we attribute their superiority to the significance of their content, the depth and scope of their conflict, or the relevance of their action to the major aspects and problems of humanity. In tragedy, there is always a precipitate of final enlightenment—some inherent cumulatively realized, understanding. We have seen an experience enacted on the stage, and have externalized its

inner counterpart in ourselves by the process of vibrating to the acted passions; or possibly by some other means, since unconscious processes are open to infinite debate. Then, ensuring the externalization of the inner drives we have given them form and meaning—that is, understood their causes and effects, which brings us to the furthest point from the unconscious, or from nebulous emotion, ever reached by the individual. Enlightenment, is, therefore, the third component of the process of purgation.[51]

Finally, we can maintain with Gassner

that enlightenment is not only the third element in catharsis, but the decisive one. The ultimate relief comes when the dramatist brings the tragic struggle to a state of rest. This cannot occur so long as we are left in a state of tension. No matter how well the action or the main character's destiny is resolved and concluded, the anarchic forces, "the pity and fear," evoked by the tragedy cannot establish a suitable inner equilibrium. Only enlightenment, a clear comprehension of what was involved in the struggle, an understanding of cause and effect, a judgment on what we have witnessed, and an induced state of mind that places it above the riot of passion—can affect this necessary equilibrium . . . . Only enlightenment can therefore round out the esthetic experience in tragedy, can actually ensure complete esthetic gratification. True tragic exaltation, which we require of a tragedy, also lies in this. For the exaltation comes only if we have prevailed over the anarchy of our inner life and over the ever present and ever pressing life around us. And how can we master this anarchy without understanding it, without putting order into this house of disorder?[52]

CODA

The word *catharsis* in Greek has more than one connotation and more than one of these has been applied by scholars and critics over time to Aristotle's use of this term as the climactic point of his definition and theory of tragedy. The thrust of the argument that I have developed here is that the only nuance of the word that can be persuasively applied to Aristotelian tragic theory and in any meaningful approach on our own part to the encounter with great tragedy and great literature in general is by recognizing catharsis in these circumstances in its truly authentic cognitive role and function as "intellectual clarification." It was in Plato's *Sophist* that we were told that the greatest of all forms of catharsis was the Socratic process of challenging all propositions with a rigorous sequence of question and answers until cognitive certainty was attained or declared unattainable. I have argued that it is this tough-minded spirit of intellectual discovery that controls the role of catharsis as Aristotle uses this term in his analysis of tragedy's meaning and goal. This is also why the act of literary criticism at its best is also a powerful intellectual act of discovery as can be seen in this penetrating judgment by E. R. Dodds on the hero of *Oedipus Rex*:

> But surely the *Oedipus Rex* is also a play about human greatness. Oedipus is great, not in virtue of a great worldly position—for his worldly position is an illusion which will vanish like a dream—but in virtue of his inner strength: strength to pursue the truth at whatever personal cost, and strength to accept and endure it when found. "This horror is mine," he cries, "and none but I is *strong* enough to bear it" (1414). Oedipus is great because he accepts the responsibil-

ity for *all* his acts, including those which are objectively most horrible, though subjectively innocent.[53]

This act of analysis certainly accomplishes for us a climactic moment of what John Gassner has designated as "enlightenment." Moreover, Gassner correctly evaluates "enlightenment" as the "decisive" component of catharsis [crediting the emotional turmoil stemming from tragedy's driving emotions, pity and fear, with being two subordinate components]. He attributes to this dominant factor of enlightenment in catharsis, and it alone, the power of evoking a sure comprehension of what was contained in the struggle and turmoil of the tragic plot, that is "an understanding of cause and effect, a judgment on what we have witnessed and an induced state of mind that places it above the riot of passion;" then he adds "only enlightenment can therefore round out the esthetic experience in tragedy, can actually ensure complete esthetic gratification" (Gassner 1965, 110–11). What Gassner has accomplished here is to spell out in specific detail and in the language of a great drama critic what was foreshadowed some 2,400 years earlier by the cognitive aesthetics of the philosopher Aristotle, who declared that "the act of learning is not only most pleasant to philosophers but, in a similar way, to others as well, only they have an abbreviated share in this pleasure. *Thus, we find pleasure in viewing representations because it turns out that we learn and infer* [manthanein kai logizesthai] *what each thing is*" (*Poetics*, chapter 4—my italics). This view was reinforced much later by the great twentieth-century German/American classical philologist Kurt von Fritz whom we cited earlier in this study. Now at an appropriate point in our survey of important cognitive intepretations of catharsis, we provide also the German text of his deep insight. He stated that catharsis did not have only an emotional aspect but in accordance with

Aristotle's view, "it is more 'philosophical,' meaning that it leads to deeper insight, than history, and its cognitive function is of equal importance to its emotional effect" ("Die Tragödie ist nach Meinung des Aristoteles auch 'philosophischer,' d.h. zu tieferer Einsicht führend, als die Geshichte. Ihre Erkenntnisfunktion ist also ebenso wichtig wie ihre emotionale Wirkung").[54] In the same passage, he further emphasized this point when he added that Aristotle had attributed to tragedy the capacity to provide insight into the universal principles governing the human condition (durch die von Aristoteles nicht minder hervogehobene durch die Tragödie bedingte Einsicht in ein καθόλου, ein Allgemeines, die allgemeinen Bedingungen der *condition humaine*).

In his informative 1979, and still relevant, survey of competing interpretations of catharsis, Donald Keesey comes to the following conclusion:

> It occurs to me that there are several advantages to the term clarification in this context not the least of which is one that Golden himself might hesitate to acknowledge. I refer to the ambiguity of the word or, if you like, its shiftiness. It won't stay put. So in one sense Golden admittedly follows Else by placing catharsis in the text, and in a similar sense he agrees with Kitto and Goldstein that it is a process applied to the incidents by the very act of mimesis. In quite another sense, however, the catharsis would appear to be operating on the audience, our understanding is clarified. And sometimes it seems to be even an operation performed by the audience . . . .
>
> As far as I can see, Golden, in his various presentations of his view, does not seem to be aware of this fruitful ambiguity; at any rate he never specifically remarks upon it. Nevertheless it is there, and I think it is a positive advantage which inheres in the very term "clarification." The mime-

sis clarifies the incidents in such a way that the audience is able to infer the universal from the particular and to receive the pleasure which comes from learning. Through artistic representation, our emotions are "intellectualized" and mastered . . . . To editorialize, the mimetic process clarifies the materials to create the poetic structure; the poetic structure, in turn, clarifies our understanding.

To my mind, Golden's approach has many virtues. Like Kitto and Else he is concerned to assert the unity of the Poetics, but his reading of the key phrase is even more fully integrated with the rest of treatise. Further, the implications and overtones of the word "clarification" are consistent not only with Aristotle's formal emphasis but with Aristotle's generally "intellectualist" approach. The pleasure derived from mimesis is the pleasure of perceiving . . . . of learning, and the translation of catharsis as "clarification" fits much better than the other alternatives with the widely held opinion that Aristotle's famous definition does seem to say that catharsis is the end or goal of tragic art.[55]

We recall that the history of the interpretation of catharsis as the cognitive dimension in our experience of tragic mimesis began, as far as I can tell, with correspondence between two German scholars in the early decades of the twentieth century. That correspondence did not lead immediately to any revolutionary change in the traditional ways in which catharsis had been understood. It was a half-century or more later, quite independently of any previous antecedents, that momentum for an important paradigm shift in catharsis interpretation began to develop persuasive force. From the mid-twentieth century on different scholars, arguing from different vantage points, contributed evidence and justifications that could be used to support a cognitive interpretation of catharsis. Now, early in the

twenty-first century, we have an important affirmation and aug-
mentation of the line of reasoning that had been energized in the
previous century. Professor Christopher Shields in his comprehensive and authoritative survey of Aristotelian thought writes:

> From this vantage point, artistic activity is continuous with
> scientific activity. On Aristotle's approach, poetry and the
> arts are for something and what they are for is not very
> different from what our scientific endeavors are equally, in
> the end, for. Art and Science, supposes Aristotle, find their
> purpose in human knowledge-seeking activity; we humans
> by nature desire to know--and we come to know by studying
> and producing, by theorizing and spectating, by experienc-
> ing and reflecting. So, finally, we are engaged in and by the
> arts for the very reason we find ourselves engaged in and by
> science; we do so because we are humans.[56]
>
> Catharsis would then be, perhaps, clarification. The mem-
> bers of an audience reach emotional clarity by purifying
> both the cognitive and affective dimensions of their emo-
> tional states; and they might do so by purging such states of
> their unhealthy or illicit components. Catharsis is not the
> end of tragedy, but one means among others for modelling
> human character. The function of this modelling in turn,
> is not some sort of emotional purgation, as if a tragedy is
> successful just when its spectators leave the theater depleted
> and ready for bed. On the contrary, tragedy *leads to under-*
> *standing* (my italics) and understanding to right action. The
> success of tragedy resides not in catharsis; rather, catharsis is
> successful when it serves the ends of tragedy.[57]

I agree with much that Shields says here but I think that
there is a significantly better way than his to describe the relationship between tragedy and catharsis. First, we know with

precision that for Aristotle the goal of tragic mimesis is to facilitate learning and inference (Gk. *manthanein kai sullogizesthai*) about the real world experiences that are the subject of the artistic representation. If, second, we accept the developing argument we have traced for interpreting catharsis as "clarification," then tragedy and catharsis come to have exactly the same cognitive goal. The two concepts are seamlessly and reciprocally embedded in one another.

Over the centuries, Aristotle's *Poetics* has received much attention and praise. It is time to pay the *Poetics* its full measure of respect by recognizing the authentic and abundant contribution it has made to the humanistic tradition of Western civilization by no longer obscuring its key term, catharsis, with trivializing accolades associated with speculations about "medical purgation" and "moral or aesthetic purification." The *Poetics* represents a potent strategy for accessing literary tragedy, one of the great repositories of the "wisdom" literature of our culture that exposes the forces in our society that are responsible for much human suffering that, on different occasions, its victims endure with impressive courage or fall victim to because of moral or intellectual frailty. The *Poetics* does not offer either cure or palliative for human tragedy but only a clarification of its ubiquitous reality.

ENDNOTES

1   This term (Gk. *mimesis*) is translated in English as representation or imitation.

2   See I. Bywater, *Aristotle on the Art of Poetry* (Oxford: New York, 1980 [1909]) ad loc. 1448 b 16. Other scholars have noted this "cognitive" or "Platonic" influence on Aristotelian mimesis. J. A. Elias attributed to Plato both a "strong" and "weak" defense of poetry. The weak defense of poetry sees mimesis as a methodology open to those who cannot muster the rigor for a dialectical quest for ultimate truth. The strong defense of poetry, he says, "is quite another matter, as it deals with the capacity of forms of *mimesis*—metaphor, image, myth—to establish productive axioms, for further, more rigorous, inquiry." Of the success of *mimesis* in this regard he tells us: "it is successful, as any set of axioms is successful, not because it is true, but because it has explanatory power, it is fruitful in generating consequences (theorems) that accord with experience and intuition, and forearms against experience not yet encountered." See J. A. Elias, *Plato's Defence of Poetry* (London: Macmillan, 1984), 226, 230.

3   This term (Gk. *hamartia*) is translated variously in English as failure, failing, fault, to err, to miss the mark, and so forth, as discussed in the ensuing paragraphs.

4   See G. Crane, "Composing Culture," *Current Anthropology* 32 (1991): 293–311.

5   Bywater, *Aristotle on the Art of Poetry*, 215.

6   D. W. Lucas, *Aristotle: Poetics* (Oxford: Clarendon Press, 1968), 143. On the general meaning of *hamartia*, Lucas writes, "the basic idea is to be found in the verb *hamartanein* 'to miss the mark, to err, to fail.' From it are formed two nouns *hamartia* and *hamartema* which in many senses are indistinguishable . . . . Thus, a man under the misapprehension as to the identity of his parents would suffer from a *hamartia* which might lead him to commit a *hamartema* whenever he took any action relating to his real or supposed parents." See Lucas, 299–300.

7   This term (Gk. *aretē*) has various meanings and is translated in English as virtue, goodness, excellence, good service, distinction, and the like.

8   This term (Gk. *spoudaios*) is translated in English as good, excellent, fine.

9   See I. Bywater, *Aristotle on the Art of Poetry*, 155, ad loc. 1449 b 27.

10   See among others L. Golden, *Aristotle on Tragic and Comic Mimesis* (Atlanta: Scholars Press, 1992); S. Halliwell, *Aristotle's Poetics* (Chapel Hill: University of North Carolina Press, 1986); D. Keesey, "On Some Recent Interpretations of Catharsis," *The Classical World* 72 (1979): 193–205; P. Laín Entralgo, *The Therapy of the Word in Classical Antiquity*, ed. and trans. L. J. Rather and John M. Sharp (New Haven, CT: Yale University Press, 1970); B. Simon, *Mind and Madness in Ancient Greece* (Ithaca, NY: Cornell University Press, 1978).

11   G. F. Else, *Aristotle's Poetics: The Argument* (Cambridge, MA: Harvard University Press, 1957), 440.

12   P. Laín Entralgo, *Therapy of the Word*, 230.

13   Kurt von Fritz, *Antike und moderne Tragödie* (Berlin: Walter de Gruyter, 1962), xxvi.

14   D. Keesey, "On Some Recent Interpretations of Catharsis," 197.

15 L. Golden and O. B. Hardison, Jr., *Aristotle's Poetics: A Translation and Commentary for Students of Literature* (Gainesville: University Press of Florida, 1982), 295.

16 Sophocles, *Oedipus Rex*, Revised Edition, ed. R. D. Dawe (Cambridge, UK: Cambridge University Press, 2006 [1996]), 1.

17 *Ibid.*, 2.

18 *Ibid.*, 3.

19 D. Birge, "The Grove of the Eumenides: Refuge and Hero Shrine in *Oedipus at Colonus*," *The Classical Journal* 80, no.1 (1984): 11.

20 The Editors of Encyclopædia Britannica, "Irony," *Encyclopædia Britannica*, 2007, accessed March 21, 2017, https://www.britannica.com/art/irony.

21 E. R. Dodds, "On Misunderstanding the *Oedipus Rex*," *Greece and Rome*, second series, 13, no. 1 (Apr. 1966): 43.

22 *Ibid.*, 47–48.

23 *Ibid.*, 48.

24 *Ibid.*

25 A. C. Bradley, *Shakespearean Tragedy* (New York: Penguin, 1991), 36.

26 *Ibid.*, 36.

27 *Ibid.*, 37.

28 *Ibid.*, 181.

29 A. Miller, *Death of a Salesman*, in *Collected Plays, with an Introduction*, Viking Critical Library, ed. Gerald Weales (New York: Viking, 1996 [1967]), 144.

30 *Ibid.*, 147.

31 John Gassner, "Essays on *Death of a Salesman*" in *Death of a Salesman*, *ad loc.*, 235–36.

32   John Mason Brown, "Reviews," in *Death of a Salesman, ad loc.*, 208 and 209.

33   A. Miller, *Death of a Salesman*, 144.

34   A. Miller, *Collected Plays, with an Introduction* (New York: Viking, 1996 [1967]), 164–67.

35   Citations of Miller's observations in the following paragraph are taken from, *Collected Plays, with an Introduction*, 167.

36   Bernays's argument first appeared in *Grundzüge der verlorenen Abhandlung des Aristoteles über Wirkung die Tragödie* (Breslau: n.p., 1857); later reprinted in *Zwei Abhandlungen über die aristotelische Theorie des Drama* (Berlin: n.p., 1880).

37   D. W. Lucas, *Aristotle: Poetics*, 276–78.

38   S. O. Haupt, *Wirkt die Tragödie auf das Gemüt oder den Verstand oder die Moralität der Zuschauer?*, oder, *Der aus den Schriften des Aristoteles erbrachte wissenschaftliche Beweis für die intellektualistische Bedeutung von "Katharsis,"* Bibliothek für Philosophie, 12. Bd. (Berlin: L. Simion, 1915). 18, http://catalog.hathitrust.org/api/volumes/oclc/15238490.html. A translation of the title of this work itself shows that this article introduces the concept of understanding catharsis as intellectual clarification: The Effect of Tragedy on the Feeling or the Understanding or the Morality of the Audience? Or, The Furnishing of Scientific Proof from the Writings of Aristotle for the Intellectual Meaning of "Katharsis."

39   L. Golden, "Catharsis," *Transactions and Proceedings of the American Philological Association* 93 (1962): 51–60.

40   L. Golden, *Aristotle on Tragic and Comic Mimesis*, 37.

41   R. P. McKeon, "Literary Criticism and the Concept of Imitation in Antiquity," *in Critics and Criticism: Ancient and Modern*, ed. R. S. Crane (Chicago: University of Chicago Press, 1952), 166n.

42   M. C. Nussbaum, *The Fragility of Goodness* (Cambridge, UK: Cambridge University Press, 1986), 388–91.

43 Golden and Hardison, *Aristotle's Poetics*, 92–93.

44 Aristotle associates pity and fear in literary tragedies with mimesis, as is evidenced in chapters 4 and 6. The entire first paragraph of chapter 4 (1448b4–17) requires us to interpret "through pity and fear" as meaning "through the mimesis of pitiable and fearful events." He shows this in his definition of tragedy in chapter 6 (starting at 1449b24), "tragedy is the mimesis of a noble (or serious) action . . . . through pity and fear achieving the catharsis of such emotions (or experiences)." This is a literal translation of the beginning and ending of the definition that Aristotle gives of tragedy in chapter 6.

45 O. B. Hardison, Jr., "Commentary on Chapter VI," in Golden and Hardison, *Aristotle's Poetics*, 116–18.

46 *Ibid.*, 151–56.

47 See Nussbaum, *Fragility of Goodness*, 388–91.

48 See L. Golden, *Aristotle on Tragic and Comic Mimesis*, 64.

49 *Ibid.*, 265–66.

50 B. Simon, *Mind and Madness*, 143-45.

51 J. Gassner, "Catharsis and the Modern Theater," in *Aristotle's "Poetics" and English Literature*, ed. Elder Olson (Chicago: University of Chicago Press, 1965), 108–13; essay originally published in *One Act Play Magazine and Theater Review* (August 1937). Mr. Gassner lived from 1903 to 1967, and the article in which this quote appears was published in 1937, a time when the terms "purgation" and "purification" were the most commonly accepted ways of rendering the Aristotelian term Gk. *katharsis*. As argued in this book, over the second half of the twentieth century a paradigm shift was gaining in momentum in which I and several other scholars and critics laid the groundwork for rejecting the then common translations of "purgation" and "purification" as acceptable explanations of Aristotle's use of catharsis in the *Poetics*. Our arguments, cited in detail in this work, demonstrate

that those rejected translations of the Greek term *katharsis* clashed sharply with Aristotle's explicitly expressed theory of tragedy. In their place, we argue for substituting a proven and well-founded nuance of the usage of *katharsis* in Greek philosophical and epistemological texts. That is, the preferred understanding should be "intellectual clarification," or a synonymous variant of it, which is fully in harmony with Aristotle' core argument in defining the nature of tragedy. Readers of Gassner's present essay would likely agree that if he had the opportunity to follow the arguments that were developed after his death in favor of understanding Aristotelian catharsis as "intellectual clarification" he would have welcomed them with enthusiasm.

52 *Ibid.*, 110–11.

53 Dodds, "On Misunderstanding the *Oedipus Rex*," 48.

54 K. von Fritz, *Antike und moderne Tragödie*, xxvi.

55 D. Keesey, "On Some Recent Interpretations of Catharsis," *The Classical World 72 (1979): 202–3.*

56 C. Shields, *Aristotle,* 2nd edition (New York: Routledge, 2014), 465–66.

57 *Ibid.*, 458–59.